Esodus:
Internal Reflections
And
Conversations With The Sun

Asar Imhotep
(The Black Lotus)

KALA BA NGANGA

MOCHA-VERSITY

A MOCHA-Versity Press Book
www.mochasuite.com
www.mochaversity.com

Interior and Cover Art Computer Graphics: Harold Johnson
Editing: Chaz Kyser

LCCN: 2007941948

ISBN: 978-0-6151-7875-2

If you move forward
You're going to die
If you move backwards
You're going to die
You might as well move forward and die!

****

When death comes knocking at your door
Let him find you living!

—*Dagara proverbs*

Contents

What is my purpose?

What must I do to fulfill that purpose?

Acknowledgements

I would like to take this opportunity to acknowledge some key people who have made this work possible in some manner. I must first acknowledge my ancestors, those named and unnamed, who have paved the way and on whose shoulders I stand. Without their sacrifice I would not be here today to tell a scratch of our story—a story that certain members of the human family have vehemently tried to suppress.

I would also like to thank my MOCHA Suite Phamily who have been with me throughout the years and have contributed in making www.mochasuite.com a place where people can come and get food for thought that tastes good and provides vital nutrients for the mind, body and soul. Those members are Tory Carmon, Lasana Hotep, Dexter Gabriel, Chaz Kyser and Mark Smith. There are also people who are close to you, who know just how lazy you really are but refuse to let that prevent you from receiving your blessings. For me that person is Evette Branham. Without her getting on my derrière, this project would have probably never been completed, at least in this decade. Thanks for the support.

There are many others whom I can't possibly name who have in some manner shaped my thought process, so please forgive me if I do not acknowledge you here. But I would like to take this time out to honor those who have challenged me and helped me to refine my thought process while encouraging me to think big and to go back through our history and find the necessary tools to build a new reality for generations to come. These persons are Dr. Jim Conyers (University of Houston), Steve Mackey, Chris Brown, Jabadi Powell, Dr. Julani Williams (RIP), Akua Holt, Minister Robert Muhammad, Baba Alaafia, Baba Oshofu, Okomfo Kimati Dinizulu, Professor James Smalls, Asa Hilliard III (RIP), Dr. Molefi Kente Asanti, Abiodun Oyewole, Ashra Kwesi, Brother Taha, Dr. Malidoma Some, Todd Smith, Paul Eeasterling, Rev. Johnny Youngblood and Deloyd Parker.

I would also like to thank all of the poets who have supported me throughout the years and helped to improve my writing and performance: Se7en, Terrence (Mean Joe Swanson), Punkin From Pluto, Marcell Murphy, Marie Brown, Tosha Terry, Black Snow, Black Bluez, Black Poet, Blaque Ink, Brother Said, Angie G, PJ, Saida, Khimmy J, and L'Avation.

Last but not least, I must acknowledge my son, Elijah Heru Johnson, for whom all of my sweat and tears are for. The foundation is for you to build upon; take it and run with it.

Introduction

"Kani ka bwe, kana ku lumoso-ku lubakala-ku n'twala-ku nima-
mu zulu evo mu nsi ukwenda, vutukisa va didi I yand."

"No matter what, you may walk leftwards, rightwards, forwards,
backwards, upwards or downwards,
you must come back to the core/center"
—Ba'Ntu Kongo proverb

The above quotation was taken from the definitive work of Dr. Kimbwandende Kia Bunseki Fu-Kiau's *African Cosmology of the Bantu Kongo* in the chapter on the Bantu concept of the "Vee" (to be explained below). This proverb summarizes in the Kongo language what I have truly come to believe regarding my own convictions in life. *Esodus: Internal Reflections and Conversations with the Sun* is really a journal, a diary of philosophical ideas from my comparative studies in history, philosophy, meta-physics, spirituality, cultural anthropology and from watching movies, living life, and day dreaming when I should have actually been doing some work. The more and more I began to study and write papers and engage in conversations with master teachers from around the world, the more I began to realize that at some point, one has to come to one's own convictions in life based upon his understanding and research.

Often times we go through life believing, with no contest, other people's convictions, even when they run contrary to our own. We do not feel our thoughts, our ideas, our questions and our solutions are comparable to others because we did not go to the right schools, did not get initiated into the correct spiritual systems, or read the right books, etc. This limited mode of thinking has prevented some human beings from realizing their full potential because they fear being different. They fear being ostracized by authorities, family and friends because they do not necessarily think in the

1

traditional ways. They devalue their worth in the social community of ideas because they are afraid to challenge orthodoxy. Now don't get me wrong, I am a firm believer in you doing your homework and knowing at least the basics before formulating an opinion. Too many times we have seen people voicing their opinions without a logical foundation to stand on. This book is a challenge to readers to write down and voice their own opinions so that they can leave their intellectual footprint in the cosmic sands of time.

This "Age of Aquarius" (the Zodiacal information age) is a good time to be living. One of the major challenges for historians is getting an accurate picture of a society during the time period of study. For those societies who have left written records, we usually get a one-sided view of how things were going in that time period. Very few people in ancient times could read or write, so the stories and philosophies of the average citizen are forever left to speculation. Reading and writing were left to the elite, so the average citizen was represented in history by a class that may not have had their best interest in mind, or really understood the mindset of those who made up the working class, and their personal histories, philosophies, and ways of seeing the world. Ancient Ta-Meri (Egypt) is a perfect example. Because of this, we often speak of a collective personality while ignoring the varied personal convictions of that community. Our understanding of that society is slightly distorted because certain variables are missing in this complex social equation.

What we are used to in Western schools of education is a linear, one-sided, long, self-congratulatory narrative of Europe's entry into history and how its great ancestors made the world "a better place." Europeans took advantage of the world's alleged "illiteracy" and falsified history to suit their economic needs. But as more people, Africans in particular, began to get educated in *their* systems, we began to uncover a history as ancient as time itself. Who we thought were the creators of civilization, were in fact indebted to those very human beings whose history they tried to erase.

This age of Microsoft Word and the internet have afforded people with the ability to tell their own stories in a manner consistent with their own level of consciousness. No longer will we have records on the state of the world by just the society's elite and political conquerors. This prevents future members of the world community from distorting history for their personal gain. A new day has come when man has confidence in himself and his abilities to shift the social consciousness to create a reality in which the dominant culture exists to help the collective human personality forever reach higher echelons of awareness.

This brings us back to our Kongo proverb at the start of this introduction. To feel at harmony with our convictions, we must always come back to the self and see how the information we obtained from speculative inquiries or empirical observations can help us fulfill our destiny (if you believe in destiny). I believe at the time of writing this book that we are aspects of the *Supreme Creative Force* of the Universe.

This *creative force* created this *Matrix* (as expressed in the Matrix films) so it could have experiences. I believe that human beings are the central nervous system of this creative force and we send messages to the creative force to make it aware of its current condition and just how far it needs to go to fully understand who and what it is. When we meditate and reflect on the events of the past, we are engaging in a ritual that allows the supreme creative for to understand itself through the human experience.

To truly understand the proverb, you must understand the Kongo's concept of the "Vee." If you pay attention to the cover of this book, you will notice a figure of a Mu'Ntu (human being, person) standing center of two planes: a vertical plane and a horizontal plane. Graphically, this represents the trajectory the sun makes around the earth and is symbolically applied to the lives of human beings as second *suns*.

According to Fu-Kiau, we are "Vertical-Horizontal" beings; we stand "upright," we think, reason and ponder before moving "horizontally" on the earth to meet the challenges of the instinctive world. The horizontal world is the main ground to all learning. Moving horizontally serves one purpose and that is to learn from one's environment. We are not born with knowledge. According to the Bantu, we explore and collect data from our experiences in the world. We shelve this information in our consciousness, like living computers, for future use at will. The muntu has two planes of motion in this universe. On the horizontal plane he can move forwards, backwards, leftwards and rightwards. These movements are for learning and collecting information. The vertical plane is critical to his health and self-healing. On the vertical plane he can walk upward and downwards. But for true self-knowing (Rech Ib – Know Thyself) he walks inwards [didi – inner world]. This is the location of his true self, the essence of his being, his connection to the source and ancestors. The Bantu of the Kongo believe that a muntu deminishes his self-healing power unless he discovers how to walk towards this seventh direction. The journey towards the didi makes us "thinking-acting-beings," doers, masters [nganga] to ourselves.

When we lose our ability to have experiences within ourselves, we lose our self-healing power. Part of our job as human beings is to help other human beings walk towards this center. This journey of self-discovery not only empowers the muntu, but restores him as a whole by turning on his self-healing power, which in turn activates the *order-giver-stimulus*. A full examination of the Bantu concept of the "Vee" would take a whole volume to even begin to give it the kind of attention it rightly deserves. But I will attempt briefly to further explain how this concept relates to the formation of this book.

Since spirituality is predicated on our ability to "see," I must again refer you to some visuals so one can better grasp the traditional African concept of the "Wheel of life" in which the Bantu concept of the "Vee" becomes clearer.

I was introduced to this cosmograph [Fig.1] in various other African spiritual systems starting in ancient Ta-Merri (Egypt). Those familiar with Dr. George GM James' work, *Stolen Legacy*, will no doubt recognize the following graph.

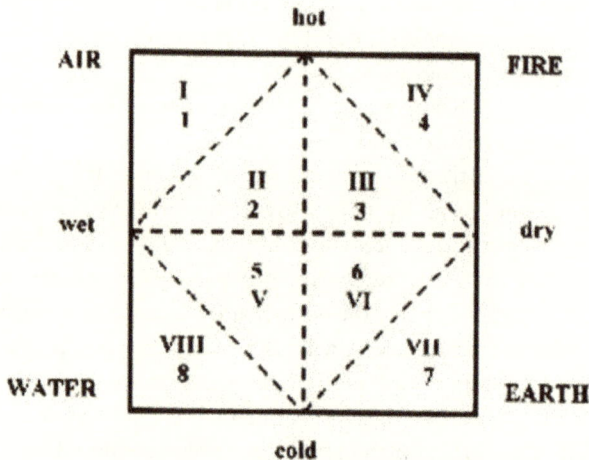

The Four Elements: AIR, FIRE, WATER, EARTH
The Four Qualities: HOT, DRY, WET, COLD
The 8 EQUAL POLE STARS

[Fig. 1]

Above is the diagram of the *Law of Opposites* from W3st (Waset, Thebes) and is a graphical representation of the cycle of life. Overwhelmingly, traditional African thought sees human beings (ba'ntu) as "living-dying-living" beings. This means there is a cycle to life and our spirits are reincarnated to have new experiences. The conversations I've had with priests from all over Africa, and my own personal accounts and studies, have led me to believe that most, if not all, major spiritual systems in Africa can be traced to the Twa & Bantu people in Central Africa. What we have is a story of migrations over a long period of time in which priests made settlements in different parts of Africa. These settlements never lost their tie to their ancestral home and as time progressed and the settlements got bigger, these villages became just as old as the original ancestral home. As hundreds and thousands of years went on, a few migrants went on to explore other parts of Africa and the world, bringing their concept of culture and spirituality with them. As a result of these migrations, you begin to see the same spiritual concepts, although slightly altered, as part of the new culture that arose at later times in history. The meaning and iconography are practically unchanged within these settlements and a few examples will be given to prove the point. The same cosmograph you saw in ancient Ta-Merri (Egypt) you will see in Benin with the Vodun practitioners, with some of the same names as will be explained later on in this section.

[Fig. 2]

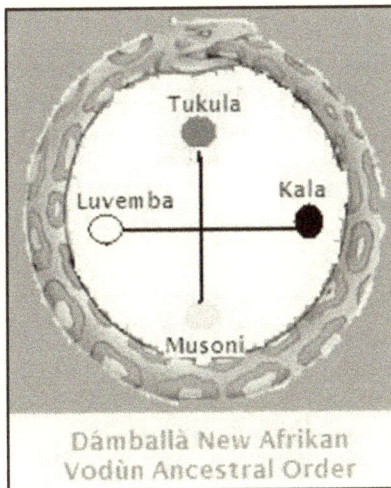

Dámballà New Afrikan
Vodùn Ancestral Order

Pay attention to the following graph and keep it in mind
when we start talking about the Bantu concept of the "Vee."

[Fig. 3]

The above is a "Veve" (symbol) for one of the Loa (energies, Orishas,
Netchers, Obosom) of Damballa in the Vodun tradition of West Africa. Pay
attention to the structure of the "V's" throughout this image.

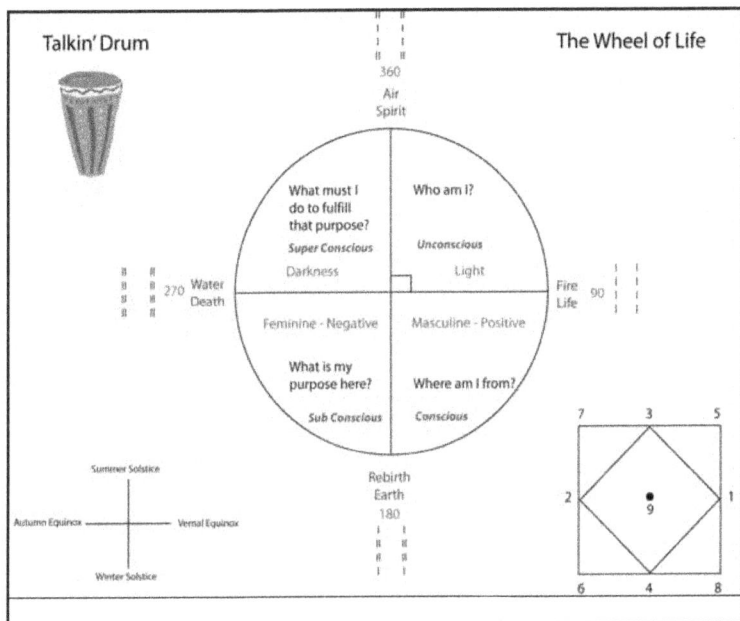

Talkin' Drum   The Wheel of Life

360
Air
Spirit

What must I   Who am I?
do to fulfill
that purpose?
Super Conscious   Unconscious

270 Water   Darkness   Light   Fire 90
     Death   Life

          Feminine - Negative   Masculine - Positive

What is my
purpose here?   Where am I from?

Sub Conscious   Conscious

Summer Solstice   Rebirth
                                   Earth
Autumn Equinox ———— Vernal Equinox 180

Winter Solstice

7   3   5

2   1
         9

6   4   8

[Fig. 4]

Above we have a representation of the same graph, with more detail as to its meaning in the spiritual system of Ifa. This is a graph I created for a local study organization called *The Talking Drum* headed by Babas Femi Fayimi and Shango Dari. In each of the above diagrams, there is a circle broken down into four 90 degree angles, which form a "V" shape. Each section in all of the systems represents a stage of life or a stage in initiation. It serves other purposes as well but they are outside the scope of this lecture.

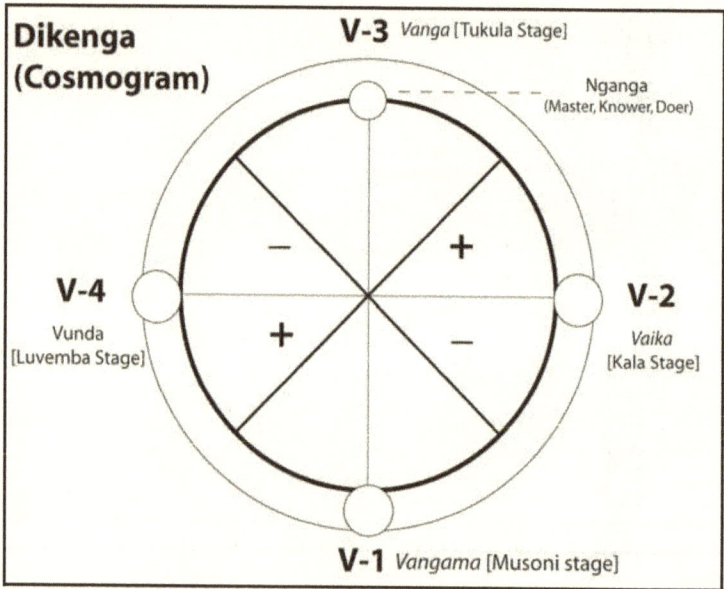

Dikenga (Cosmogram)

V-3 *Vanga* [Tukula Stage]

Nganga (Master, Knower, Doer)

V-4
Vunda [Luvemba Stage]

V-2
Vaika [Kala Stage]

V-1 *Vangama* [Musoni stage]

[Fig. 5]

Above is the Bantu Cosmogram (Dikenga), which is the source of all of the above graphic philosophies. The Bantu believe that human beings are living "suns" forever on a course of living-dying-living. This process of "re-re births" follows a spiral trajectory that you can see through these graphs (figures 5 and 6. Each section of the graph represents a different stage in this life process and is critical in understanding the African world view. The first "V" is called *Vangama*; it is the biological formation process stage (the womb). This is where all of our genetic codes are imprinted [sonwa] into the future "living sun." This is also a symbolic reference to the place where all ideas are born. Ideas follow the same process of development human beings do, and in the cosmic womb, the mind is where we impregnate consciousness and give birth to new ideas. This is where you get the idea of the Mers (Pyramids) developed in Sudan, but made famous in Ta-Merri. V-2 is called *Vaika*. This represents the actual existence stage (the birthing process) in which you become a breathing, sound-making [vovi] being. You now have the ability to code and decode the world around you. Your ability to speak

[vova] allows you to make, receive or reject orders (the order-giver stimulus spoken of earlier). This ability can either curse you or bring you good health. This speaks to the power of words.

V-3 is the most aspired "V" of any muntu. It is the *Vanga* stage and is derived from the archaic word "ghanga," which means to do or perform. This "Vee" is the stage of maturity, creativity and great deeds (the *tukula* stage). Inventions and great works of art are all developed in this stage. At this point one becomes an Nganga (a master, a true knower, a doer and specialist in the community). This is a person who stands "vertically" (for all of you Masons) in his own "V." This is a reversed pyramid and occupies the position of verticality [kitombayulu] in the directions of Gods, power and leadership. For those of you who have studied Nile Valley history, this should all sound familiar and graphically it should all make sense now. The Egyptian "Ankh" symbol is none other than a man standing vertically in his own "V." Notice all of the top priests carried one with them. It was considered the "key of life" and now one should be able to "see" what they meant. It was also a level in the priesthood that George GM James points out as the "sons [suns] of light." A person who stands "well" in this zone not only knows himself, but his relationship with the rest of the universe as a whole as well (see figure 6 below).

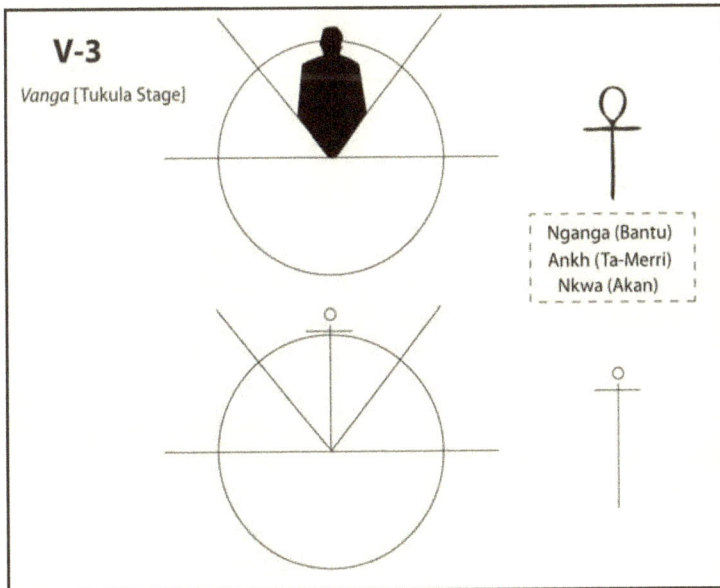

V-3

Vanga [Tukula Stage]

Nganga (Bantu)
Ankh (Ta-Merri)
Nkwa (Akan)

The last zone in the Dikenga is *Vunda* (V-4). It represents the greatest change of all and that is death. Vunda means *to rest* and this is where you enter the realm of living energy called the ancestral realm. Here, depending on how you lived your life in the *Nseke* (world, earth), you would either be a *n'kuyu* (ugly, immature, stunted ancestor) or a *mukulu* (deified ancestor).

How does all of this relate to this work you are reading? This work is a book of philosophy and poetry. This is a journal of my current thought process and convictions as of November 2007 (age 28 for me). There are many different dimensions that make up a muntu (human being) and I am no different. I am a historian, a philosopher, graphic designer, father, software developer, an artist, a musician and most know me as a poet (commonly known as The Black Lotus).

I am also a living-energy-being going through my many stages of life trying to be an Nganga (a master, a doer, an artistic, creative being). An Nganga is always about the business of making history, leaving his stamp on life and bringing a fresh perspective to this human experience. This work is to help me better know myself.

According to Bantu philosophy, a muntu is a combination of (before birth) what both parents poured into his "me package" (genes), what the mother injected into the me-package in the womb, and (after birth), what he is fed, what he feeds himself, what he sees, what he learns/hears, what he believes in, what he does (occupation), and what is around him (known and unknown forces, radiations). I would like to inject another aspect of the human personality that if not nurtured makes a person incomplete: how a person creatively expresses himself.

Creative expression is so central to a person's make-up that without some sort of avenue to creatively articulate one's convictions, one loses his ability to heal himself as well as the community and he becomes a destructive force within society. Imagination and the ability to carry out our will are the defining characteristics of what makes us human. So in essence, if one does not have a creative outlet, then one cannot claim to be fully human. Cultivating our creative faculties is a necessary component in the realization of our humanity, so much so that it prompted Albert Einstein to say, "Imagination is more important than knowledge." He's also quoted as saying, "Logic will get you from point A to B. Imagination will take you everywhere."

Imagination is the vehicle for progress and self-development. It is the foundation for all future inventions (see *The Human Being: Universal Converter of Ideas*, pg.119). We express our creative philosophy through a thing we call "art." Art is simply the **art**iculation of our imagination through physical or audible mediums. When we engage in song, painting, sculpting, drawing, weaving, dancing, etc., we are engaging in a healing process that maintains our sanity and helps us to unveil the God within us.

One of my artistic endeavors is poetry. Poetry allows me to articulate all of my thoughts in a creative way and serves as a mnemonic device to help me recall information stored in my subconscious more easily. Poetry has allowed me to serve my community on many levels and has allowed me to turn various people on to the many facets of our great African history and philosophy.

This book is a study of poetry, philosophy, and a poet. I believe a poet is a philosopher. We are the ones who ask the pertinent questions and provide creative solutions to some of society's tough inquiries. The poet's creative mind allows him/her to "see" what others can't see. Poets are masters of speech and can speak to the hearts of a people in an effort to cause change or help society get to know itself more intimately. The poet, the Djeli, the Griot in Africa, holds a very prominent position. He is the keeper of the history. The poet evokes emotions that cause change in a society. Dr. Malidoma Some, in his book *Of Water and the Spirit*, speaks about the importance of the Griot (pg. 57). He goes on to say:

> The one experience that all humans share is grief, and it takes the right
> kind of *poetry* to set grief ablaze. This is why the griot chanter, the
> guardian of the mythopoetic doors of the tribe, is an invaluable engineer
> of emotion. (emphasis mine)

Art for the African is more than an aesthetic covering for self-expression. It holds a spiritual significance and is used as a tool to bring ashe (power) from the ancestral realm into this one to work for the greater good of the community [the *Law of Attraction* before Hermes Trismegistus and before Oprah showcased the "The Secret" back in February 2007]. Dr. Malidoma Some again expresses the importance of art in indigenous life on pg. 61:

> The magical arts are Dagara [tribe of people located in Burkino Faso
> west Africa] technology, a technology characterized by practicality—what
> is needed, what is useful. When one of our elders carves a double-headed
> serpent or an amphibious mammal, he is not just creating an image out
> of his imagination, but cooperating with the spirits of those beings for

the maintenance of the natural order. Through this carving, spirits from the underworld manifest themselves to heal us in the world above and to repair our world. To the Dagara, art is the form in which spirits choose to exist with us here in this world.

With this work I hope to achieve several things. The main thing is to inspire other human beings to fully write out their thoughts and feelings in a manner that is true to their spirit and present it to the world with no apologies. This volume is a challenge to readers to leave their own footprints in the cosmic sands of time; to do the best with what they have, at the place they're at, with the time allotted them (to be an Nganga). We must leave records for future historians to find so they can get an accurate picture of the philosophy, the culture and the events of our time. I urge others to create works of art that will serve as time stamps for reflection and understanding. Art is a medium to help you get to know yourself. Go back to your thoughts and expressions and reflect on them to see if you still believe what you believed before. An Egyptian proverb states:

> Everyone finds himself in the world where he belongs. The essential
> thing is to have a fixed point from which to check its reality now and
> then. Always watch and follow nature.

Go back to see how much you have grown since the last time you had a serious conversation with yourself and try to answer for yourself why you believed what you believed and if it is still relevant to have such convictions today. Another proverb states:

> Have the wisdom to abandon the values of a time that has passed and
> pick out the constituents of the future. An environment must be suited
> to the age and men to their environment.

Esodus: Internal Reflections and Conversations with the Sun is my journal to the public in the form of essays and poetry. This will be an anthology of work that I will reread in the future just to see if I still believe the same things I believed at the time of writing this book. If I come to a point where certain points of conviction have changed or have been altered, I will write another book with more articles and poetry to reflect my maturity (or lack thereof).

Esodus is a collection of articles I've written over the years for my website *www.mochasuite.com* (MOCHA Urban Hang Suite) and poems I've created over my lifetime. Esodus is a term I coined (or at least I think I coined the term), which is different from the more popular term "Exodus." An exodus is an "exiting," a leaving away from something [made popular in the Biblical myth]. I am encouraging readers to do the opposite. It's time we stop exoding (yeah, I made it up) and begin to look inward (to our source, our culture, our families, spirit and ancestors) for true understanding; thus the term *Esodus*. The Greek prefix "eso" means "inside," like in esoteric, and this is the challenge our ancestors left for us graphically with the Dikenga cosmogram. These are my reflections on life as a living "sun" traversing around my own personal Dikenga trying to find meaning in this experience. I hope this work sparks a process of internal conversations with yourself and points you to a path to your own spiritual liberation.

I want to make sure that 500 years from now, philosophers will know for sure that not everyone in the 21st century in the United States was a conservative, rich, "White" Christian male who tried to preserve "good ole" American values to the detriment of the rest of the world's populations and environments. I want future generations to understand that there are common folks who had ideas, who had innovations, who had a different perspective, who were creative and weren't afraid to voice their convictions and give their take on what it meant to be human.

We still have spiritual knots to tie, mountains to move and love to share. When death comes knocking at your door, let him find you living.

Asar Imhotep (The Black Lotus)
MOCHA Urban Hang Suite, 2007
Houston Ministry of Culture

References:

Fu-Kiau, K. Bunseki. (2001). *African Cosmology of the Bantu Kongo: Princples of Life and Learning*, Athella Henrietta Press
James, George GM. (1993). *Stolen Legacy*, Africa World Press
Some, Malidome. (1994). *Of Water and the Spirit*, Tarcher Putnam

Kemetic Proverbs

Massey, Gerald. (2004). *Ancient Egypt the Light of the World, Volume I*, Nuvision Publications

Schwaller de Lubicz, Ihsa. (1978). *Her-Bak: The Living Face of Ancient Egypt*. Inner Traditions

Schwaller de Lubicz, Ihsa. (1978). *Her-Bak: Egyptian Initiate*. Inner Traditions

What Is Philosophy?

When we think of philosophy here in the West, the theorists who come to mind are usually European philosophers who lived between 570 to 332 BCE, such as Thales, Plato, Aristotle, Socrates, Anaxagoras, Democritus, Zeno, Parmenides and Melissus. We must also include those philosophers of more contemporary times, such as Schopenhauer, Descartes, Baudrillard, Locke, Hegel, Kant and Nietzsche. All of these men and more have contributed greatly to our understanding of western philosophy.

Unfortunately, in universities across the world, they begin the journey of speculative philosophy with the Greeks, as if no other group of people—many who had civilizations thousands of years older than Greece—ever thought about things considered "philosophical." This has led to a devaluing of other world cultures and the raising of Europeans as the bringers of civilization and deep thought. In other words, the world was in darkness until Homer, Plato and Aristotle jumped on the scene to shed light on the human condition. Historians intentionally and systematically neglected African philosophers such as Imhotep, Kagemeni, Amenemope, Ptah-Hotep, Antef and Hor-Djed-El. The Chester Beatty IV papyrus mentions the name of such philosophers and gives reverence to these philosophers thousands of years before Greece was a political state. The Chester Beatty papyrus goes on to say:

Books of wisdom were their pyramids,
And the pen was their child...
Is there anyone here like Hor-Djed-El?
Is there another like Imhotep?
They are gone and forgotten,
But their names through their writings cause them to be remembered.

This essay will not focus on Greek philosophers and how they came to Africa to study what later became Western speculative philosophy. Warrior scholars such as Diop, Obenga, Karenga, Winters, James and Asante have proven this case in my eyes several times over. What we will delve into here is the true nature of philosophy from within the cultural context of classic and contemporary African people. What you will come to find is that philosophy is not what you have been taught in American universities (just a systematic reflection on life). It is a more practical method of development using nature as a guide to find meaning and purpose in the lives of human beings. I hope to add insight on the origins of philosophy and how the pursuit of its intrinsic characteristics can enhance our spiritual lives and serve as a model for social cohesion and human florishing.

Philosophy

Philosophy according to Webster's Dictionary is: 1) the pursuit of wisdom; 2) a search for a general understanding of values and reality by chiefly speculative rather than observational means; 3) an analysis of the grounds of and concepts expressing fundamental beliefs. This fits nicely into the cultural context of European collective thought, but is not totally in alignment with classical African thought, which heavily influenced western philosophy.

The word philosophy breaks down to its Greek roots: "philo," which means "lover," and "sophia," which means "wisdom." So philosophers are "lovers of wisdom." This implies that one not only learned about universal phenomena, but was passionate about that search. Love implies a strong desire for that in which the connection implies. This intense investigation was done in order to provide models for better living here on earth and to look for the root causes of the underlying reality in order to build a model society in which humanity may live.

The word "Sophia" can be traced to the ancient Mdw Ntr (Medu Netcher) of the Nile Valley from the word "Sba" (seba), which means to teach, school, and be wise. "Sbty" (sebaty) means pupil and a further derivative, Sbyt (sebayit), means "wisdom teaching, written teaching, wisdom, instruction and pedagogy." Seba became "sophos" in the Greek starting with Pythagoras, who is believed to have coined the term after his 22 years of study at the temple of Amen in Waset. The letter 'b' in the Mdw Ntr turns into "ph" or "f" oftentimes in the Greek. An example would be the Kemetic deity "Nbti," which turns into "Nephthys" in the Greek.

The first fundamental definition of a philosopher (or wise man) in written history comes from the Inscription of Antef (12th Dynasty, 1991-1782 BCE). The inscription has been translated by Hellmut Brunner to read as follows:

> [He is the one] whose heart is informed about these things which would be otherwise ignored, the one who is clear sighted when he is deep into a problem, the one who is moderate in his actions, who penetrates ancient writings, whose advice is [sought] to unravel complications, who is really wise, who instructed his own heart, who stays awake at night as he looks for the right paths, who surpasses what he accomplished yesterday, who is wiser than a sage, who brought himself to wisdom, who asks for advice and sees to it that he is asked advice.

This text informs us of the passion and foresight one must have to get to the root of problems; the drive one must have to surpass what he/she accomplished yesterday, not being satisfied with past accomplishments. This clearly lets us know that a *Sba* is one who actively seeks knowledge and is in a continuous dialogue with himself as he unravels the mysteries of his time. Reflection on life's events provides us an opportunity to make sense of reality and this is the prerequisite of all philosophical undertakings. With this understanding, the Sba develops a process in which his wise insight can provide the most beneficial solutions to social conflict (Isfet) and help humanity reach its full human potential.

Mdw Ntr (Medu Netcher): The key to understanding philosophy

I posit that the key to understanding philosophy from the standpoint of the African priests lies in the understanding of what Mdw Ntr is and how this played a central role in the development of philosophy, which is so often overlooked. Warrior scholar Chiekh Anta Diop has always encouraged Africanists to look at ancient Ta-Merri for understanding the culturisms of the rest of Black Africa. For Diop, Ta-Merri plays the same role for Africa that Greece plays for Europe, and with that in mind, we will look to Ta-Merri for a better understanding of the fundamental essence of philosophy as they understood it.

Mdw Ntr is often referred to in Egyptological texts as "Divine Speech." While this may give a technical definition of the term, it doesn't quite grasp the understanding the Africans had in mind. Mdw Ntr is more than a writing system; it is a philosophical approach to understanding abstract ideas. It was also a mechanism for carrying out the *Law of Attraction*[1] so eloquently hidden within its cosmic myths and Ta-Merri's architectural designs.

Mdw Ntr is the natural language of the universe. To the African, all objects in nature are really symbols for the underlying causal reality that cannot be perceived through the human senses. Objects in this realm of existence are the form of divine ideas. The creation myth written on the Shabaka stone (25th Dynasty 716-702 BCE), commonly referred to as the Memphite Theology, talks about the creator Ptah "speaking" creation into existence. Ptah uttered sounds to churn the waters of the "Nun" (primordial matter), which differentiated the oneness and gave form to potentiality.

African people wholeheartedly believe in the "Hermetic[2]" concept of "As above, so below." This means that whatever happens on a celestial level, happens on the earthly sphere. Whatever happens within the spiritual realm also has its corresponding reality within the realm of matter. To understand Mdw Ntr, you have to understand this concept as well as the creation myths of the Kemetjw (Egyptians). For each phrase in Mdw Ntr was an attempt, using the Law of Attraction, to bring celestial and spiritual events, as expressed through their myths, into the social sphere in which they lived.

Mdw Ntr writing is a symbolic, holistic approach to understanding. You can read the characters from right to left, left to right, down and even backwards. The symbols were a combination of various objects you would find in nature, as well as the tools and inventions of the times. With this understanding,   we   can   break   down   Mdw   Ntr   to   mean:

Mdw = symbolic for form (masculine, phallic symbol)

N (water) = Nun (undifferentiated matter), wave, write, create

Tj [ch sound](rope) = Guide, Bind or Bridge, Calabi Yau space

R (mouth) = Law, warp/bend gravity (matter), at, by, near to, toward, into, with

In one creation myth, Atum swallows his own semen and spews out creation[3], once again alluding to the concept of creative utterance, self-creation, and this is probably the philosophy in which the word Mdw (creative speech) is referring to. It was sound that churned the waters of Nun and gave form to it, and it is also the power of speech that shapes (forms) our reality. So every time we speak, we are actively engaging in the creative process just like the deities Ptah, Atum and Ra: each sound spoken mimics the celestial mythos-play of creation[4].

With that in mind, in African indigenous societies, they didn't have written laws. "Laws" were really a set of proverbs, unwritten taboos, passed down by ancestors. In other words, laws were passed down orally and the way you adjudicated law was through your mouth. This is why the /r/ symbol means law: it is a symbolic reference to how laws were passed down and arbitrated in African societies (see Dr. Fu-Kiau *Mbongi: An African Traditional Political Institution* pgs. 36-49) and references the creative words of power (heka) of the creator itself.

The glyph /tj/ (symbolized by a rope) means *guide* or *thing that binds*. This symbol is actually the physical representation of a Ba'Ntu philosophical concept. The Ba'Ntu believes that the universe is essentially a big ball of energy waves and radiations. As Dr. Fu-Kiau (2003: 9) has articulated:

> . . . nothing is isolated in the universe...Likewise, human beings, living or dead, as living suns rising and setting around the world, are all related to each other. The warmth of radiations never die at sunset, the physical death. *It is here that the misconstruction of the myth of the ancestors' Cult of Africa began in the Western literacy of Africa.* (emphasis mine)

In African societies, the main purpose that drives a community is the constant need for a connection with the spirit world. Spirits do not die; they simply are a part of the universal energy that permeates throughout nature waiting on its time to return to earth. Dr. Fu-Kiau (2003:9-10) goes on to state:

> African people do not worship the dead. They venerate *N'singa dikanda waninga*, the community's genetically bounding **rope** (power) strengthened between the dead and the living. (emphasis mine)

This rope is what binds the spirit world to the world of matter. It symbolically leaves a path between the two realms (like bread crumbs) and as long as this connection is not severed, the health and vitality of the community will flourish.

The /n/ symbol represents the creator as undifferentiated matter. In practically all indigenous African societies, the "beginning" is represented as a "fluidity" represented as water or an ocean. This fluidity is the "summation" of the boundless potential of creation. From this fluidity, creation came into existence when the creator emerged out of potentiality. This is the realm of stored knowledge.

The symbol for /mdw/ is a burning flame. This represents masculine energy and is another phallic symbol (as the phallus stands vertically like a flame when ready to procreate). This glyph is a metaphor for "form" as new life takes form after the sperm leaves the phallus and unites with the egg in the woman's womb. In traditional African philosophy, creation comes about through heat or the heating process (Kaa, Kali, Kala, Kalunga, KaaUma [Kmt] – meaning charcoal, to blacken, burn, mature, develop and come into being). It is a play on the transformative process used in metallurgy and alchemy to turn one type of substance from one form to another (it is how men give birth).

So Mdw Ntr is the study of the "**laws which guide the Nun into form.**" This is why they were so preoccupied with nature. Studying the laws of change in nature gave them a working model on how to construct their society. They were actively seeking a process of creating the best of what was in the spiritual realm here on earth. This is why they never abandoned the pictorial method of writing throughout their 4,000 plus years of political history. This is the fundamental difference between Greek philosophy and African philosophy: African philosophy was a way of life that can be seen in the culture, architecture, scientific pursuits and in their spiritual systems. It wasn't created for mere speculation.

The African understanding of the concept was that to understand the *unseen*, you had to study the *seen*. This is what makes the Webster's definition of philosophy inaccurate because it posits gaining knowledge "chiefly [through] speculative rather than observational means." This was not the understanding of the ancient Africans. Wisdom was obtained through the development of good character and the application of good judgment based upon what you could see (or perceive).

This gives us a better understanding of what *meta physics* is, as the word meta physics comes from the Kemetic word Mdw Ntr. Modern meta physics is a branch of philosophy that is concerned with the nature of the world: it is the study of being or reality. Some have taken it to include faith, spirits, occultism and crystal healing power, which are not in alignment with its original intent.

Linguistically, "d's" and "t's" are the same. For an example, say the letter "D" to yourself. Now say the letter "T" and notice where you place your tongue. It is in the exact same place. The only difference is the flow of air when you say these letters. We see this commonly within African-American Vernacular English, as well as Caribbean, when we say words like "da" instead of "the." In the Islands you will often hear people say "bruda or muda," instead of "brother or mother," respectively. For the youth on the East Coast, the "t" actually turns into a "v" at times. An example would be the Hip Hop term "word da muva" (word to [the] mother—meaning I swear to my mother that this is so).

In this same vein, "medu" became "meta" in the Greek. Meta came to mean "the work" or "process." Netcher is where we get the term "nature." It is the physical realm and the Greeks simply used their term physikos to represent nature (Netcher—the power behind physical objects). So meta physics is the "work after the physics," meaning the study of things after they come into being. It has the same connotation as can be seen in the Mdw Ntr, and the influences are apparent when one considers that the early Greek philosophers came to Ta-Meri to study. Philosophy was based on the notion that studying physical forms of things and how they function gives us insight into the workings of the mind of the *Supreme Being*.

African people of old generally did not believe in a "revealed" text. They did not believe that God came down and wrote truth in a book and that was the final revelation for all men to follow. God's wisdom was hidden, and you had to be a diligent student of nature to unlock its secrets. Indigenous Africans believed that the *Supreme Creative Force* speaks to man every minute of everyday, but man must learn to be sensitive enough to detect what "it" is saying. "God" speaks through symbols and God's symbols are the phenomena we see in nature. The Africans believed that the physical realm is a "multi-verse" (instead of a uni-verse). The word verse means "statement" and this again is a reference to the belief "God" spoke physical creation into existence. So your job as an initiate was to try and learn the language of God so you could actively engage in the cosmic conversation and read the literature (multi-verse—multiple statements). That's the mystery behind Mdw Ntr. This is why you used symbols to convey messages. This is why you worked on having good speech and uplifting words because the symbols and the sounds both play as magnetic devices that attract the spiritual concepts and give it form. This is Mdw Ntr—the ability to transform consciousness into "things."

The Europeans couldn't grasp this concept coming into Africa. They saw all of the carved images and saw people dancing, singing and meditating around these images and said they were "idol worshipping." This is far from the case. This was a deep spiritual exercise that facilitated the process of drawing energy from the spiritual world to shape social reality and transform potentiality into "things" that are useful for mundane tasks. Often times you will hear modern new age spiritualists tell you that if you want something, let's say a car, you have to visualize yourself already having that object. Sometimes they tell you to take a picture of what you want and keep it with you always to remind you of what you're working towards. The universe will create the circumstances so you can obtain that object and the image helps you to stay focused on the goal. You aren't worshipping the car, you are simply aiding the subconscious mind to help you focus on your goal. The belief is that the universe is creating for you what you sincerely put your energy behind and what you focus on—negative or positive. So if this is the case, one should consciously focus on the things that would bring balance and happiness in our lives. This is one of the major aspects of Mdw Ntr and this is the original intent of philosophy.

Conclusion

Philosophy was not a discourse for man to debate about whose perception of life was more profound. It was an exercise in understanding how the universe transforms ideas into "things" and how we as human beings can do the same thing. Through this spiritual pursuit, Africans were able to discover the processes of the various branches of science (physics, mathematics, architecture, music, chemistry, astronomy, biology, etc.) and use that knowledge to enhance the human condition. Our challenge is not to just reflect on the nature of reality, but to be active participants in the creation of the kind of reality we wish to have. The quality of our lives depends on our desire to learn how we can transform ideas into "things" and how we can do this in a harmonious manner that enhances the human condition and brings about human flourishing. Philosophy is the synthesis of all learning with the specified aim of increased wisdom and moral and spiritual perfection.

References:

Asante, Molefi Kente. (2000). *The Egyptian Philosophers: Ancient African Voices from Imhotep to Akhenaten.* African American Images; 1st edition.

Fu-Kiau, K. Bunseki (2003). *Self Healing Power & Therapy.* Baltimore, MD. Black Classic Press

Hilliard, Asa III. (1997). *SBA The Reawakening of the African Mind,* Florida, USA: Makaare

James, George G.M. (1992). *Stolen Legacy,* New Jersey, USA, First Africa World Press

Karenga, Maulana, (1989). *Selections from the Husia,* University of Sankore Press; 2nd edition

Obenga, Théophile. (2004). *African Philosophy: the Pharaonic Period, 2780-330 BC.* Popenguine, Senegal: Per Ankh,.

Obenga, Theophile. (1995). *A Lost Tradition: African Philosophy in World History.* Philadelphia: Source Editions.

Notes:

[1] It states that people experience physical and mental manifestations that correspond to their predominant thoughts, feelings, words, and actions and that people therefore have direct control over reality and their lives through thought alone. A person's thoughts (conscious and unconscious), emotions, beliefs and actions are said to attract corresponding positive and negative experiences, or "harmonious vibrations of the law of attraction."

[2] Hermes Trismegistus – (thrice great Hermes) is the syncretism of the Greek god Hermes and Egyptian Neteru Djehuty. He was later revived during the Middle Ages and Renaissance times by philosophers and alchemists and is credited for writing the *Hermetica*. This set of philosophy inspired a 1908 book written anonymously by a person, or persons, who called themselves "the three initiates." In this book Hermes gives seven universal laws and one of them is the *Law of Correspondence.* As above, so below.

[3] *Book of Overthrowing Apophis* - Translation and notes by Alexandre Piankoff, in his *The Shrines of Tut-ankh-amon* (New York, 1955), P. 24. Cf. the translation by John A. Wilson, in ANET, pp. 6-7

[4] Te Velde, H (1969-70). *The God Heka in Egyptian Theology*

Allen, J (1988, 38). *"Genesis in Egypt: The Philosophy of Ancient Egyptian Creations Accounts."* Yale Egyptological Studies 2, New Haven: Yale Egyptological Seminar

Coffin Text VII, 481 – A de Buck. (1935-1961). *The Egyptian Coffin Texts.* 7 Volumes. Chicago: University of Chicago Press

Leiden Papyrus I 350, IV, 6ff

Who Am I ?

Who Is The Black Lotus?

Everywhere I go, someone inquires as to the meaning behind my poet name, "The Black Lotus." First let me say that I have several names, and at any given open-mic I may use any one of these names, as it depends on what mood I'm in that day. These names include The Black Lotus, De-Mate Da Prophet, The Voice of Many Waters, Sean Maximus, Usr Maat Ra Stp M Ra Sa Ra Msw Mry Amn, **ART**imus Prime and/or Morpheus.

Although they all represent a certain personality trait, the one I introduce to audiences the most is *The Black Lotus*. This name has more meaning, to me, than the rest and speaks to the richness in African philosophy. So in this introduction, I am going to give you the breakdown, according to how I see it, as to what The Black Lotus really means.

We must start this journey in the ancient Nile Valley swamps, which were an integral part of the geography of Northeast Africa. In these swamps you can find lotus flowers, better known to botanists as *Nelumbo nucifera*, which allegedly was introduced to Ta-Merri (Egypt) by the Persians. You do, however, find native to the land what they call the "Blue Lotus" along the Nile and its current name is *Nymphaea Caerulea*. It is also known as the Sacred Blue Lily (although the Lily is a separate plant called *Agapanthus Africanus*).

People who were unfamiliar with the plant's actual growth and blooming cycles believed that the lotus flower opened in the day and sank closing below the water at night. However, the flowers open and bud during a period of two to three days, opening at approximately 9-9:30 a.m., and closing around 3 p.m.

It was a sacred flower in ancient Ta-Merri because it was believed to rise and fall with the rising and setting of the sun. So it took on mythical attributes that were symbolic for traits to be obtained by man. The aim was to always open oneself up to light (knowledge) as does the lotus. You are to rise above your circumstances as does the lily. *Nymphaea Caerulea* plants grow in murky, muddy conditions, yet they are never soiled by the environment. It has its roots in the world (the mud), but rises beyond the illusions of the world to embrace the light (knowledge). This was the job of man and this is one aspect which I adopted in the name The Black Lotus. It represents not only my true life circumstances and convictions, but my people's in general. We are known for coming from the most gutter places, yet we always, through our spirituality, show the world how to become fully human and rise above the circumstances that seem to be impossible to overcome. Slavery is a good example. Instead of coming out bitter and murderous, we came out of that situation with peace, humbleness, a sense of spirit and community. This is not supposed to happen to a people right out of slavery. Not only that, we became the fastest ethnic group in history to become literate and contribute to the collective knowledge of the nation.

The Nymphaea Caerulea plant also has been proven to have some psychoactive and physiological effects on the body. It was used as a "visionary" enhancer and was taken either by way of smoking it or brewing it in teas or alcohol (wine being the favorite). It was seen as the key to good health, sex and rebirth. The Blue Lotus was an aphrodisiac and enhanced sexual vigor like *Viagra*, was used as a pain killer like Arnica, a tonic like *Ginseng*, and circulation stimulant like *Ginkgo Biloba*. I like to think that my poetry acts as vitality enhancers for the mind that gives you the energy to make a change in your community and family. I do not want my words to just be a mental stimulant, but to be a conduit for good mental and physical health. Now, alone with my girlfriend, it could be associated with a certain vigor we know that all grown folks engage in, but that's another discussion. Because of its usage as a vehicle for ecstasy (not the drug commonly used by teens in the United States), I suspect it was also used in ritual practices to help the initiate enter a state of possession.

The Black, on a simple level, is associated with the ethnic heritage of myself and my people. Although I do not believe in the concept of biological races or color having any relation to language, land and lineage (ethnicity), I use this folk taxonomic designation to bring out something a little more spiritual. The Ba'Ntu have a concept called "kala," which means "to be, to become, to light fire." The concept itself is associated with BLACKNESS and is used as a symbol of "emergence" (coming into being). In the Kongo, man (mu'ntu) is considered a second "sun." He is to rise like the sun in order to Kala (to be). A man differentiates himself from the animal kingdom by his ability to walk upright, think and create systems. A man stands up vertically before starting tasks and moving (becoming) in any of the four cardinal directions. So you rise like the sun, like at noon time (as the sun is directly above man at this time, giving a vertical line from man and the sun), and you should be about the business of creation (Masons won't get this in the morning). Kali, Kalunga, Kaa are all Ba'Ntu words that deal with Blackness and "charcoal." The use of charcoal (blackened or charred wood) in ancient African societies had many practical uses and was used metaphorically in spiritual concepts. Charcoal is used for cooking and heating. It is also used to extract metals from orche used to make all types of things. From these processes comes the notion of *transformation*. Charcoal is used to extract metal from orche as mentioned above. In essence, it is from the heating process (the big bang of Kalunga) that life took shape in the universe as in the case of metals taking shape after the heating process of burning charcoal. It is only after the grafting process of our lower nature (as fire purges and purifies metal) that we are able to shape our character (like metal) to a state that is useful for society (like a tool: say farming - cultivate, culture).

So with all of this in mind, the Black in The Black Lotus deals with an emergence, as the lotus emerges out of the murky waters and stands vertically as the noon day sun, to reach for the light and create poetry, systems, art, music, healthy relationships, etc. It is also a reminder of the vast potential that lay dormant in the blackness of creation waiting to go through the grafting process of our minds, through our imaginations, to take shape and form here on Earth. The Black Lotus is an ideology, a reminder of what every poet should be engaged in: creating something out of nothing and giving an audience the necessary tools to get out of their murky conditions and be budding, life-giving (like plants) human beings who are always reaching for the light (knowledge) and using that knowledge to enhance the human condition. This in a nutshell sums up the meaning behind the name.

This article is respectfully dedicated to the youth who march onward and upward towards the light.

References:

Nymphaea caerulea - Water Lily / Blue Lotus
http://www.entheology.org/edoto/anmviewer.asp?a=65&z=6

Nymphaea caerulea
http://en.wikipedia.org/wiki/Nymphaeacaerulea

Fu-Kiau, K. Bunseki, (2001). *African Cosmology of the Bantu-Kongo*, Athella Henrietta Press, Brooklyn, New York

Nuk Pu Nuk (I Am That I Am)

I am that I am
I am that I am
I am that I am
I am
I am that I am

I am that I am

Born in a region of steadfastness
A place where nothing grows
No sorrow or sadness
I am that I am
Because I've always been
In this place of Bush- o-nomics
I will transcend

I am a celestial spirit whose purpose is unknown
I travel through time and space through infinite time-zones
An infinite force here with infinite faces
With infinite lifetimes and manifestations
The first time I arrived, I came as Asar
I gave man a code of ethics to help them live up to par
They couldn't handle my righteousness so they plotted my death
I was kidnapped and murdered by my own brother Set
But I didn't fret, no, I still had life left
I came back as Aha Menes, united all of Egypt

I built pyramids and sea ships and circumnavigated the world
I plotted star constellations and watched the Milky Way swirl
The Hyksos invaded, so I mounted a defense
I came back as Ahmose I and I haven't seen them ever since
I exploited my resources until there was nothing left to gain
I came back as Queen Hapshetsut when there wasn't a man to reign
I began the process of agriculture and science I mastered it
The world was in trouble so I was reborn in Nazareth
I carried the world on my shoulders and it came with a price
But after my ascension yo they labeled me Christ
Just a little bit north I saw the behavior was foul
So I came as an African by the name of Bilal
I gave them tenants and statures and a spirit to draw from
I gave them spirituality and they renamed it Islam
Constantine had a conference in which they were scheming and plottin
I came back as St. Augustine and gave them sound doctrine
The Hebrews made a claim that I had enslaved them
They suddenly had forgotten all of the knowledge I gave them
They called me Ramesis II, but got the name wrong
My name is Usr-Maat-Ra Setep-en-Ra

And I am ....
Born in a region of steadfastness
A place where nothing grows
No sorrow or sadness
I am that I am
Because I've always been
In this place of Bush-o-nomics
I will transcend

I appeared at time in which whites had despised me
I came as Beethoven but Blacks couldn't recognize me
By this time I already navigated the north shores
I heard Europe needed civilizing, so I came as the Moors
Up in the Americas Europeans were frontin
My people needed a savior so I came as Harriet Tubman

They attempted to put my freedom on stall
I created a brotherhood under the name of Prince Hall
I survived the Middle Passage, I survived through Jim Crow
I survived the Depression, I survived through disco
The list goes, on of my many manifestations
I came back as Parliament Funk and created one nation
Under a groove—I helped civil rights to move
I came as Marcus Garvey and helped Universal Negroes Improve
I survived through the lynching, I survived through perjury
The doctors needed help so I performed the first open heart surgery
The Egyptologist told me about Kemet's white skin
So I had to set the record straight and came back as Dr. Ben
But they still weren't convinced, so I yelled from the tree-tops
I performed melanin tests on mummies under Cheikh Anta Diop
I went from jazz to be-bop, from poetry to hip hop
I came in the form of Dizzie Galespie and left as Tupac
I came as Malcolm X to expose the cowards
I came as Huey Newton but they couldn't handle my Black Power
They looked at my afro and unification in amazement
The personification of strength when I arrived as Angela Davis
I am an infinite being with an infinite purpose
There is no telling under whom next will I surface
I could reincarnate here as your daughter or son
There's no telling from which direction I'd be coming from
Spirits don't die my peeps, they only change form
If you could only understand the journey I'm on

Cuz I am ....
Born in a region of steadfastness
A place where nothing grows
No sorrow or sadness
I am that I am
Because I've always been
In this place of Bush-o-nomics
I will transcend

Pitch Black

I'm so Black
That I play skip rock with slave bones and create
    hurricanes in the Atlantic Ocean
So Black, I can make my hips move to the rhythms of celestial commotion
So Black that when I do a sermon
    I can make fixing a sandwich sound empowering
I'm so Black that I make cows lactose intolerant
As Queen Hatsheptsut, I ruled Egypt without a husband
Every time I beat box, I summon the spirit of Harriet Tubman
And she leads the charge against modern day hip hop minstrel shows
In my early years I used primitive bow and arrows to hunt Jim Crows
I walked on water with white Adidas shell toes
And hell froze over when I wrote *The Parable of the Sower*
I'm so Black
    That I turn Shaolin fighters into *Thelonius* Monks
So Black that the government in England will turn into a *Parliament* Funk
Black like power fist picks and afros
Black like grand mamma telling you to close that damn screen doe(or)
Black like slamming bones during dominoes
Black like little Black girls with they lip smack and neck rolls
Black like Amenhotep
Black like Alpha Phi Alpha
Black like pouring out libations
Pitch Black like after the rapture
That Mufasa Black
That James Earl Jones, Barry White, Don Cornelius type Black
That playin the dozens type Black
That you so Black you leave fingerprints on charcoal type Black
Black like Nkruma
Black like outfits made by Puma

Black like Dr. King, the greatest dreamer
Black like Sim Zima who got the keys to my beama
Black like We Shall Overcome
Black like don't forget where you came from
Black like you better fight when someone talks about ya moms
Black like goat skin Djembe Drums
Black like when the streets lights are on, inside you better come
Black like when you see the cops, rudebwoy you better run
Black like this Black poem is the Truth
Black like Star Wars and "I AM YOUR FATHER LUKE!"

Now how Black *is* you?

Let Me Love You The Way That I Know I Can

Why don't you let me
Love you the way that I know that I can
When I'm with you, I feel like more than a man
You are a Godsend

...Oh how I prayed
And I longed for this day
When God would send a blessing my way
So let me...

Until now
I didn't know the meaning of purpose
Until I saw this tall, curvaceous
Model who broke the mold
Lo and behold a Goddess anointed in Egyptian oils
With skin as rich as African soil
Her smile is so bright that she makes the Sun squint
If she isn't the essence of perfection
Then she's 99.99%

(fast forward)

My life took on a whole new meaning when I met you
Even if I had amnesia, there's no way I could forget you
You are a love architect the way that we build
On conversations about Africa and how we can rebuild

Because I know you have my back, there's no need for fronting
You remind me of Harriet Tubman
The way you went back into the depths of hell
In the Underground Love Road
And rescued my sense of faith, optimism and passion
And you never lost a passenger
And all of this just from a smile in passing
And your garment I'm grasping
Trying to release these demons from relationships past
My heart's been broken and you were the first to sign my cast
And you just got that gift of gab
The first woman to make me laugh
I love the fact that you are patient
I even love when we argue about little stuff in our conversations, like
..Neo? Girl you know Morpheus was the true star of the Matrix!..
It's nothing but smiles on our faces
When we're at the restaurant holding hands saying graces
And as we express love in public places
I dig your sales technique and I like what you're offering
All I know is I see God in you and I bring to you burnt offerings
Giving thanks for the day you walked into that Café
At that time
When I was there
From the minute you walked in I couldn't help but stare
And I was almost blinded by the glare
The way the sunlight reflected off the cuticles of your hair
And I swear
You are my Earth and I your moon following your orbit
Spinning on your axis
And I can't get past this . . . feeling
And those layers of insecurities you've been peeling
Back, and my soul you've been penetrating
So for life's journey I must make preparations
You are my Genesis and I get Geeked at your revelations
We be deep like Black folks and Blue Magic Grease
When with you, I feel at peace
And this poem is the least
I can do

Until I say . . . I do . . .
And we jump over that broom that swept me off my feet
And can't no other woman compete
They aren't even in the final leg at the track meet
All I'm saying is, I love how you complement me
And my only intentions are simply to treat you the best I can for as
long as you let me

So let me
Love you the way that I know that I can
When I'm with you, I feel like more than a man
You are a Godsend

...Oh how I prayed
And I longed for this day
When God would send a blessing my way
So let me...

Why I Am For The Separation Of Church And State

This essay was written for an undergraduate class in 2003 after a Supreme Court judge orderd Alabama Chief Justice Roy Moore, in August of the same year, to remove a massive Ten Commandments monument he installed in the Alabama Judicial Building.

It seems as if man's quest for spirituality has come under fire these past few weeks with the issue stemming out of Mobile, Alabama concerning the Ten Commandments being placed outside of a government building. Supporters for placing the two ton stone symbol of the Bible and the Ten Commandments outside of the Alabama Judicial Building proclaim that by placing this monument outside the building, they are somehow "Restoring the Foundations" of this country.

They act as if justice is going to be any better because a stone tablet is placed outside the courthouse. This brings up a very important question concerning what battles we choose and their value over other issues. To be brief, it wouldn't matter if the symbol is there or not. It is a representation of a deeper reality, not the reality itself.

My issue with the supporters who want to place the symbol outside the building is that they have no sympathy or understanding of other people's culturalistic views when it comes to this subject. It is my intent in this article to try to bring to light the reasons state government and religious institutions should operate separately.

Greater Religious Freedom

Because of the First Amendment, which states that Congress shall "make no law respecting an establishment of religion," people have the opportunity to practice whatever religion they choose while not being condemned by the government for doing so.

Those who disagree usually are people who do not know much about history and the Christian church. It was the Christian church in 1492 under the Pope that sanctioned slavery of Africans because they "had no souls." They made it their mission, under GOD, to civilize a civilized nation of people and in the process make money to build their civilization. Under this era of Christianization, Africans have been raped, murdered, enslaved and denied every basic human right under the sun.

This was allowed because the Catholic Church was the government of Rome. Even when the Bible made its King James debut in 1911, the poor were not allowed to read it and in most cases were jailed for doing so. Why was this allowed? Because it was a governmental body that put it into law to do so.

There are a lot more deadlier and gruesome stories about state sanctioned endorsed religion, but it would be too much for this article to mention. Just know some foul shit has been done under the name of religion.

This is why the Pilgrims and the Protestants (PROTESTing the Catholic Church) came over here in the first place. They were catching hell in Europe because they couldn't practice their form of worship under the law. Their daring move turned out to be a blatant contradiction since these same people came and murdered the indigenous people and the Africans in hopes of converting them to the "TRUE" religion of the Earth. The First Amendment also keeps the government from establishing a state sanctioned, standard religion across the board. That means you can still be Christian and not be forced to be Catholic if you are Methodist.

Symbols and their many interpretations

A symbol is a pictorial icon that represents something else. For example, the United States flag is a symbol that represents all 50 states, but the flag itself is not the 50 states. The flag was simply created to represent the states and its core value systems.

People are too caught up on symbolism. The people in Alabama are making a big deal equating the removal of the symbol with the removal of all the laws that are already on the books. That is erroneous and illogical. What these people fail to see is the bigger picture at hand. What does this symbol mean to people outside the Christian world? How was this symbol used on other people (does Constantine come to mind?). They are inconsiderate to not think about other people, especially people of color, and how they might feel concerning this symbol of the Ten Commandments. When I see the Bible and the Cross, I have a totally different perception than most in the faith, based on Christianity's violent history towards Blacks. Also, there is no evidence to support any of the historical events in the Bible, so why should I be forced to believe the events in a book that may or may not be true?

Supporters claim that the nation was founded on Christian principles and evidence supports just the opposite. "It is a sad day in our country when the moral foundation of our law and the acknowledgment of God has to be hidden from public view to appease a federal judge," said Moore, who was suspended by the Alabama Judicial Inquiry Commission for refusing to obey Judge Thompson's order.

Thomas Jefferson, one of the framers of the Constitution, discussed his belief about the separation of church and state in a letter to the Danbury Baptist Association. He states in the letter that:

> Believing with you that religion is a matter which lies solely between Man & his God, that he owes account to none other for his faith or his worship, that the legitimate powers of government reach actions only, & not opinions, I contemplate with sovereign reverence that act of the whole American people which declared that their legislature should 'make no law respecting an establishment of religion, or prohibiting the free exercise thereof,' thus building a wall of separation between Church & State.

He understood that separation of church and state was needed to prevent people who were not a part of the status quo (main religion) from being discriminated against and abused. Christians fail to realize what any symbol of Christianity means to others. Let's look at the case in South Carolina concerning the Federation Flag outside of a government building. The people who advocate its placement claim it is only a representation of their "Southern" heritage and it reminds them of a time when "their" core values were prominent. They say it had nothing to do with racism.

On the contrary, Africans in America saw this as a mockery to their existence. Because during this time, they were being shot, hung, and Black women's bellies were being cut open and photographed for postcards. This flag had a totally different meaning to these Africans. To us it seemed like the government supported slavery and the lynching of Black people and we did not want to be taken back to a time in history that overtly oppressed

Africans' right to life, liberty and the pursuit of happiness. While whites did-n't see it that way, Blacks surely had reason for opposition.

This is the issue with any religious symbolism endorsed by the govern-ment in a nation that supports freedom of religion. My child should not be forced to pray in school to a Christian God if he/she is a Muslim. As a Hindu or practitioner of Voudon, I would not think I would get a fair trial in court because they have an already preconceived notion of my character based on my religion and ethnicity.

When it all boils down to it, this is a matter of race and culture. Christianity is associated with White ideology and culture. Not only would people have a problem if a Muslim, Buddhist or Egyptian symbol was out-side of a court, they would probably sue the government for doing so since this country was supposedly founded on Christian principles. Since these religions are practiced by people of color, America would have a problem.

Separation of church and state does not equal anti-Christianity

Separation of church and state has been misunderstood to mean "against Christianity." This is far from the truth. Separation of church and state allows you to be a Christian and not be forced by the government to adhere to a spiritual system, its symbols or ideology that you do not approve of. It also doesn't allow for powerful sects who have been in existence for long periods of time, who have had a long period to recruit members, to domi-nate the scene politically and force their will on the minority. It is called checks and balances. History has proven time and time again that man, reli-gion and politics do not mix. Not only does it not mix but it can be deadly.

Asar (Entry For Encyclopedia Of African Religions)

Overview

Asar (Wasiri, Assur, Osiris) is an ancient Kemetic (Egyptian) deity (a central one in mortuary rituals) whose center of worship, or study, was in 3bdw (Abju – Abydos) in the 8th Nome of Upper Ta-Merri (Egypt). In Kemetic myth, he is ruler of the underworld (Dwt, Duat) and is the personification of the resurrection principle. He is also associated with agricultural renewal.

He is one of the main figures in the myth, which includes Aset, Heru, Set, Nebthet, and Anpu. The story contained in this myth (commonly called the Asarian Drama) is the basis for many rituals and festivals and is alluded to several times in the Prt m Hrw (Book of Coming Forth by Day). Asar became a central figure in priestly life and his shrine is located in one of the oldest predynastic cities in Ta-Merri (Anu – Abju – Abydos).

Origins

Many have speculated as to the origins of Asar. The most prominent explanation is that he was imported from Waset (Thebes) and brought into Anu. Asar is not attested to by name until the fifth dynastic period in the Pyramid Texts. The probable antiquity of many of the Pyramid Texts makes it plausible that he was recognized at an earlier period, perhaps under the name Khenti Amentiu (Lord of Amenta or Lord of the perfect Black (Amen – hidden – blackness).

A central element of the later Asarian myth, the pairing of Heru and Set, is attested from the middle of the First Dynasty, antedating the first attestations of Asar by six centuries or more. Abbe Emile Amelineau, a French

Egyptologist, discovered a series of tombs in present day Om El Gaab (Anu) in which the Tomb of Asar was found. This makes probable the notion that Asar may have been a real person who was later deified by the people of Kemet.

Over the centuries the temple of Asar was successively rebuilt or enlarged by Pepi I, Ahmose I, Thutmose III, Ramses III, and Ahmose II. Statuettes of Asar have been found as far down as the Shaba providence of Zaire.

Centers of Worship

• Abju, 8th Nome, Upper Egypt
• Saqqara, 1st Nome, Lower Egypt - to Asar-Ka & Aset
• Hut-Heryib/Athribis, 1st Nome, Lower Egypt
• Djedu, 9th Nome, Lower Egypt
• Taposiris Magna west of Alexandria, Lower Egypt
• Djan´net Tanis, west of 19th Nome, Lower Egypt
• Bigeh by Philae island 1st N, Upper Egypt
• Waset, 4th Nome, Upper Egypt, at Karnak there were five chapels built to Asar and a small temple to Asar-Heka-Djet

Depictions

The earliest depictions of Asar are of his head and torso on a block during the 5th dynasty of King Izesi. Above it is his name written in Mdw Ntr (Hieroglyphics) of an eye (Iri), which means "to do" or "to make,' and of a throne (As).

He is often depicted in human form, usually in a white or black color. Oftentimes he is depicted green as a symbol of the resurrection principle in agriculture. At times he is in Wi (mummy) form with his arms protruding out holding the signs of kingship: staff and flail. The Atef crown (White) of upper Kemet is also associated with Asar.

The Djed or Tet symbol is used in association with Asar. Djed usually means "stability" or "steadfastness." The Djed pillar is the earliest known symbol associated with Asar and may actually be predynastic. In the Rau Nu Pert M Heru (Word Utterances for Coming Into Enlightenment – *Book of Coming Forth by Day*) it is said that the Djed pillar is the vertebrae of Asar.

Some believe that the pillar is actually a pole in which grain was tied. It is often seen used in decorative friezes together with the Ankh and Was sceptre hieroglyphs, but just as frequently with the 'Tyet' knot, a symbol of Aset. This may be the reason Asar is often spelled Wasiri as his early depictions included the Was sceptre.

Asar was also associated with the Sahu or Sah (Orion) star system of the southern sky. Sahu is a constellation in the equatorial zone, visible to the naked eye thanks to its brilliant stars, which form a quadrilateral enclosing a shape like a "T."

Myth

According to Kemetic mythology, Asar was murdered by his brother Set then brought back to life by the love of his sister and wife, Aset. The love of Aset is symbolic of regeneration and the promise of eternal life. The cycle of destruction, death and rebirth was repeated each year in the annual flood of the Nile, the river that provided the essential ingredients needed to sustain life, giving birth to one of the first civilizations.

Asar and Aset had a son named Heru. Together they represent a holy family: god, goddess and divine child. In the New Kingdom, the main temples throughout Ta-Merri venerated a holy family modeled on the Asar, Aset and Heru triad.

Plutarch describes him as a human king who taught the craft of husbandry, established a code of laws, and bade men to honor the "gods" or practice ancestor worship. During initiations, initiates would take on the name of Asar in addition to theirs (i.e. Asar Ani) as a way to associate themselves with the dead king. Mystery plays used to be enacted in honor of Asar and were celebrated by the common people (although some rituals were reserved for the priests in the temples).

Ceremonies and Festivals

- The 1st Epagomenal Day is the birthday of Asar
- 25th Thuti - Asarian Mysteries
- 13th Paopi - Day of Satisfying the Hearts of the Ennead
- 16th Paopi - Feast of Asar
- 19th Paopi - Ceremony of Raising the Djed Pillar

- 30th Paopi - Kemet in festival for Ra, Asar and Heru
- 12th Hethara - Asar goes forth to Abju
- 11th Koiak - Feast of Wasir in Abju
- 12th Koiak - Day of Transformation into the Bennu Bird
- 13th Koiak - Day of Going Forth of Het-Hert and the Ennead
- 14th Koiak - Coming forth of the Bennu transformed
- 12th Koiak - Raising the Djed Pillar
- 30th Koiak - The Ennead feast in the House of Ra, Heru and Wasir
- 18th Tybi - Going forth of the Netjeru of Abju
- 17th Mechir - Day of keeping the things of Asar in the hands of Anpu
- 6th Pamenot - Festival of Jubilation for Asar in Per-Asar
- 28th Pamenot - Feast of Asar in Abju
- 30th Pamenot - Feast of Asar in Per-Asar; The Doorways of the Horizon are opened
- 30th Parmutit - Offerings to Ra, Wasir, Heru, Ptah, Sokar and Atum
- 18th Payni - Wasir Goes Forth from His Mountain

How Did You Get Your Voice To Sound Like That?

I was recently asked a question that left me perplexed and amazed
This is a frequent question and is asked more so when I come off stage
From spitting verses and stanzas and lines and riffs
Haikus and sonnets and rhymes remixed
I said, "Excuse me miss!" cuz I was taken a back
She said, "I don't mean no alarm, you just got that knack"
In a Jamaican pose of attack
With a slight arch in her back
She asked

"How did you get your voice to sound like that?"

I went into the deepest recesses of my mind, of my adolescent history
For some this question has always been a mystery
With a voice as strong as *Listerine*, it's quite hard to miss
I really began to wonder how my voice began to sound like this
I trace it to the first time that I began to study
Mrs. Byrd's 6th grade geography class and social studies
When I first began to learn the plight about African people
How we were drug on slave ships when we were down and feeble
See, instead of the weight of my heart, my voice got heavy
With each new revelation of our struggle, my voice got heavy
When I heard about COINTELPRO and the Tuskegee plot
My voice began to drop and went down a notch
When I heard about slave codes and how they kept our families hostage
My voice began to deepen and went down two octaves
When I heard of Emmitt Till and how our rights were dismissed

By this time my voice had sunken deep into the abyss

But instead of getting pissed, the universe began to channel my energy
Gave me a pen to write and improved my memory
I was visited in a dream by an Egyptian Poetry God
He said you've been given the tools and insight to be the next demigod
I've given you a voice in which people are forced to pay attention
But here's one more bit of information before I make my ascension
You must use your powers for right and for goodness' sake
When you've reached that final level
    you'll be able to make mountains shake
So now when I speak, I speak with conviction
For all of those ancestors whose voices were partitioned
And buried in unmark graves and left for not
This voice represents an amalgamation of experiences
    in which the school books forgot
So whenever I speak, my words will not be in vain
This is for Cheikh Anta Diop and Dr. George GM James
For Harriet Tubman, Prince Hall, and Marcus Garvey
Malcolm X, Marvin Gaye and Bob Marley
As my voice revs like a Harley, mimicking hard thunder claps
I marched on Capitol Hill with the weight of my ancestors on my back
And before they can kick me out the White House
    and their goons could attack
The senate asked

"How did you get your voice to sound like that?"

I take a deep breath and blow out forest fires during the summer
I pick my teeth with lightening bolts and I gargle with thunder
I eat tornado funnel clouds as if it was candy
I sip hot water from Old Faithful as if it were Brandy
I was baptized in waters of tsunami wave crashes
I practice my *do rae me's* to the pitch of avalanches
I make mountains shake with the sounds I create
I practice Egyptian yoga to the sound of earthquakes
I am the background sound to salsa meringue

I lay on beat machines and rest my head on djembes
If I'm feeling kind of down and I need to take a *toke*
I climb upon erupted volcanoes and inhale the lava smoke
I do voice overs for movies, you might recognize my sound
I play the rumble of the buildings as they're about to come down
I don't mean to boast or brag, but did I forget to mention
I received an Academy Award for best lead as a jet engine
I speak my name into a mountain and carve steep river valleys
I constantly get kicked out of libraries cuz they say my voice carries
My voice wasn't created in a lab, it was created in a dungeon
I used to have singing contests in the Rockies against Paul Bunyan
And when the set was jumpin and it was all said and done
He was like, *Fe fi fo fum*, **where'd you get that voice from?**

Nsasa

I am of the strong belief that words shape one's reality. When one fully understands the essence behind words, one's perception of life expands. People often are turned off by "semantics" in discussions. I, on the other hand, embrace using correct word usage in discussion because it helps us to better orient our thinking towards better solutions for whatever problems we are trying to solve. What's frustrating in debates is when the opposing parties get agitated at the direction because proper definitions of concepts were not properly defined in the beginning. Because the two arguers are not on the same page, the discussion becomes fruitless and nothing is accomplished. Language and perception are not different things in my opinion. The reason why it is difficult for adults to learn a second language is because they have to change their perception, their way of seeing the world. For example, the Russian language has a discontinuous tense, meaning that a concept continues, stops and then continues again. This method of tenses allowed Russian mathematicians to better deal with dividing by zero: derivatives. This method proved to be superior to the Western European methods and allowed them to win the "space race" putting Sputnik into orbit first. The Russian "perspective" made solving certain problems easier than the American's because of how they saw the world expressed through their language.

At some point in time, many of us have thought we truly understood a word until we looked at its etymological roots, and after its discovery, got a better understanding of the word and how it is currently metaphorically used. For instance, when we think of the word religion, we often think about a set of rituals by shamans, holy books, holiday celebrations or better yet, a set of rigged rules passed down by God to govern the morality of a people. While these are characteristics of some well known religions, this was not the intent of the first users of the word.

The word religion is composed of the Latin prefix "re," which means, "back, again" + "legare," meaning "to tie, bind, yoke or fasten," as well as the Indo-European root "leg," meaning to "collect," from whence the Greek "legein," and the Latin "legere," meaning "logic,' and "legal" derive. The word implies a process aimed at "tying, binding or yoking" back something that has been scattered that was once unified, as we can see with the prefix "re" meaning "back or again." This is truly a philosophical thought process as most religions believe that the essence of man and the spirit of God were unified at one time in history and then at some point became separated. This is why a "religion" was created to help man reunite with its source.

Understanding this word from its etymological roots changes our whole perspective of what religion was then in comparison to how it is practiced now. Also implied in its definition is the concept that this process is achieved by "logic," which some spiritualists claim is not the purpose of religion (saying it's all intuitive—have faith). Remember that "leg" in "legare" and "legein" means "logic" or to "collect."

Both of these words imply a gathering (collection) of facts that allows one to come to logical conclusions on matters dealing with spirit. And since "facts" can only be obtained by sensory perceptors, this means that this is a process of the study of nature (meta-physics), further stating that we deduce information about the unseen based upon the seen (physical realm). This is why you have religious "cults," as in "occult." These were organizations that helped you to "see" the hidden or unseen. The prefix "oc" (from the Indo-European "oqw") means to see.

All of this to emphasize that, as the philosopher John Locke observed, many of the academic squabbles that obstruct advancement in human knowledge could be prevented by careful attention to the meaning of words. This is why in prison Malcolm X was given the dictionary to learn before the Bible or the Koran. A person who has a thorough understanding of words and their meanings has the power to shape reality as he/she sees fit.

What is Freedom?

This leads us to the purpose of this article. In my reflections of the struggles of African people here in the States, and the many methodologies experimented for its realization, I began to wonder about what our real goal in our struggle was. What did we really want? In some circles, certain people will say that integration after the Civil Rights Movement was the biggest mistake for "Blacks" economically because segregation forced African-Americans to create and support their own businesses. Segregation led to thriving communities and opportunities not obtainable in "White" communities for African-

Americans. The communities began to suffer as these restrictions were lifted and "Blacks" moved out of their neighborhoods to live amongst "Whites," taking their businesses away as well.

It is understood that "Blacks" were fighting for basic human rights, but a term that was being thrown around at the time, which I think confused the movement, was the term Freedom. Many of you may say that this is a basic human goal that we fight to obtain and maintain for a more balanced society and personal cultivation. I am willing to argue that freedom is one of the root causes of all of humanity's major ills. Well, what do you mean? This is where the proper definition of words helps to shape our reality. I personally think "Black" people haven't realized their primary social goal because we are confused as to what the goal is. I firmly believe that we truly get what we ask for and unless we are clear about what we ask for, some undesirable results can occur. To get started in this discussion, let's define what freedom is.

Freedom, according to dictionary.com:

- A right or the power to engage in certain actions without control or interference: "the seductive freedoms and excesses of the picaresque form" (John W. Aldridge).
- Ease or facility of movement: loose sports clothing, giving the wearer freedom.
- Exemption from an unpleasant or onerous condition: freedom from want.
- Exemption from the arbitrary exercise of authority in the performance of a specific action; civil liberty: freedom of assembly.
- Frankness or boldness; lack of modesty or reserve: the new freedom in movies and novels.
- Liberty of the person from slavery, detention, or oppression.
- Political independence.
- The capacity to exercise choice; free will: We have the freedom to do as we please all afternoon.
- The condition of being free of restraints.
- The right of enjoying all of the privileges of membership or citizenship: the freedom of the city.
- The right to unrestricted use; full access: was given the freedom of their research facilities.

Although the term is applied metaphorically in many ways, the root meaning of the word is "unrestricted," and "free from restraints." My argument is that this is not what we want for human beings at all. With freedom, human beings are free to do what they want with no fear of consequence or restrictions barring them from exercising their will on others. If I saw your car and I wanted it, with Freedom, I could just take it from you with no consequences because there is no fear of consequence for my behavior.

History has proven that human beings (on an individual and societal level) do not operate on the same level of consciousness. What hurt African people the most at the beginning of European colonial times was that they couldn't conceive of human beings enslaving and torturing other human beings in the manner Europeans did. We couldn't imagine that a human being would hang a pregnant woman in public, cut open her stomach, let the fetus drop to the ground and stomp on it while taking photos for post cards. African people couldn't begin to conceptualize such a heinous act against another human being.

Europeans act the way they act because they felt/feel that they do not have to answer to anyone for their actions. Europeans have gotten away with so much in the world because very few individual states have the collective power to physically oppose their will. Europeans operate under the preconceived notion that they are free to roam the earth and do as they please without permission from the other inhabitants or with respect to the environment itself. Europeans have freedom and we don't want them or anyone else to have freedom. Freedom is undirected energy. Freedom is entropy on the social plane. What we essentially seek is a fair social construct that will allow restrictions and consequences depending on the severity of the action. For this reason, I feel that the term freedom is inadequate and I have coined the term Nsasa in its place.

Nsasa

When I came to this realization, I tried to look for a word that summed up what we really wanted in a society, but I couldn't find one. The closest thing I could find was the ancient Egyptian term MAAT, which means justice, order, reciprocity, harmony and balance. Although the deeper implications of these words can lead to an understanding of what we want, it didn't formally state exactly what we really want.

I didn't want to have to go through a philosophical discussion when trying to express what I want in this society. It should be clear and concise and there shouldn't be too many ways to interpret it.

Nsasa is a term I made up; it has no etymological roots in any other language. There might well be a word Nsasa in another language, but at the time of this article, I am unaware of such a term and this is the first word that came out of my mouth when I was thinking of a word for the concept in which I am about to explain.

> **Nsasa:** social mobility to advance and sustain one's self as a human being, in full cooperation and support of the population, where all actions are mutually beneficial to all parties involved, where unharmonious actions determined by the society have consequences equal to the offense.

In my opinion, this is what we are really fighting for. We really do not want human beings to be able to roam the earth and do as they please without feeling responsible to themselves, the society and the environment. We want others to be able to bring into fruition their wishes as long as it is not to the detriment of other human beings. Everyone involved must mutually benefit from the actions and all relevant information about the action and its consequences must be known to all parties involved. This is the basis for determining right or wrong, which has been addressed in another article.

Some may wonder why I didn't include being responsible to God for their actions. I purposely left it out because human beings are clever. They can say that you can't prove the existence of God because you can't see him/her/it. Why should I be responsible to something I can't see? But it will be very hard for someone to argue that they themselves, other human beings or the physical environment, do not exist. That should be more than enough to dead the argument. Some might still try and argue philosophically using the theory of Quantum Mechanics, but that is so pushing it.

I think that if African-Americans understood in full what they actually want from this society, we would better be able to come up with solutions that would help us realize our goals. Freedom is not what we want and frankly it is impossible to get. This is why in no society do you have freedom. Freedom is chaos. In all societies you have laws and ways of enforcing those laws so that balance and order are maintained in that society. So we should stop fighting for things that are impossible to obtain. We should clearly define our goals and make sure they are attainable in the first place. If they are not attainable, then we are wasting our time. Getting rid of "evil" is another one of those fights. The law of opposites guarantees that evil will exist because we have a term called "good," which is its opposite. Things only exist in this realm because there is a counter principle to compare it to. Getting rid of opposites would destroy creation, which makes trying to get rid of all "evil" on earth impossible.

So if we can't get rid of evil, what should we do? All we can do is try to protect ourselves from "evil," so that if we are face to face with "evil" then we have methods in place in which its effects do not affect us as much as if we didn't have these mechanisms in place. When "evil" and "freedom" are combined, we have a serious problem. But Nsasa gives us a goal to maintain and sets the framework for coming up with solutions to deter such behavior. It doesn't guarantee entropy will not find its way into the social fabric of the society, but Nsasa gives us a measuring stick by which to judge such situations.

A change in words is a change in perspective. When we realize that words are vehicles/symbols that carry a message, and we fully understand what that message is, we can better orient our consciousness to create a path for that goal's realization.

I Need A Woman
With Some Talent!

I am a young cat and I have had my share of love interests in my lifetime. When I was young, I used to have mad requirements and qualifications for women to possess in order for me to consider dating them. I kid you not, women had to be Brazilian, Jamaican, Puerto Rican, could sing, could break-dance, cook, knew Kung-Fu, had a job, wore a natural hair style, not too light, not too dark, loved dance-hall music, and could freestyle. I have matured beyond the shallowness of my teenage years. But one thing I do desire in a woman, which I find very valuable in a relationship, is the cultivation and usage of a talent.

Webster's Dictionary defines talent as:
2 archaic : a characteristic feature, aptitude, or disposition of a person or animal; 3 : the natural endowments of a person; 4 a : a special often creative or artistic aptitude; b : general intelligence or mental power.

The possession of talent in a relationship is a very important asset to have. The cultivation and usage of one's God given talents can do so much for a relationship as far as strengthening bonds and keeping it exciting. When you are into your talents, you discover a lot about yourself and it allows your mate to discover a lot about you. A problem I have been encountering in my relationships lately are females who SEEM to not possess any talents or do not cultivate their talents (afraid to be self-expressive). I know, some of you reading this will state that everyone has some sort of talent. To an extent I agree. But if you ask a woman in what manner do you express yourself creatively, and she says NOTHING, then all I can do is assume she has no talent of any kind. I have been told this by various sistas and it begs me to ask, "What is it about you that is special enough for me to pursue a long-term relationship with you?"

A talent can be anything. A talent is a skill developed from practice of a passionate interest of yours. You can sing, dance, draw, paint, research, build, joke, step, write, come up with business models, put electronics together, have a nack for community development, critique movies, carve, sow, or philosophize metaphysical phenomena. Pretty much, if you can perfect it, it can develop into a talent. In high school, I would always date girls that could sing. It was never on purpose, it was just that every girl I dated could sing. So I got used to dating girls that could sing. I am into music. Back then you could check my partner Tafiq (Tek Da Ill Shepherd) and I (De-Mate Da Prophet) either break dancing or emcee battling cats at lunch time. Oftentimes you would find females in the mix. It was always nice to be around females who were as into music and the music industry as we were. It gave us a common point of reference to initiate a relationship (whether friendly or spousal).

Here's where the problem lies: if I am a person with many interest and talents and my spouse is not into many things, then the relationship is centered around me and what I'm going to do next. I would always get into arguments about time with a few girlfriends of mine. I am a busy person, and to be with me you must know that time is of the essence. I am always into something. I am into community development, spoken word, hip hop music production, research and lecturing, dancing and computer software development. I have a talent for each one of those things I mentioned. I am always putting on social events and if any of you have put on an event before, you know that until and during that event, you don't have much time for anything as you are taking care of business to make sure the event is successful.

With this said, I for one, would like to go and do things that my WOMAN is into. Not stuff she simply likes to do, but that she is involved in herself. I want to go to her dance auditions and plays. I want to go to her concerts at a featured event. I want to see and learn from her research in anthropology, religion or African history. I want to hear her at an open mic poetry set. I want to go to her book signing, or a lecture that she is putting on at the university. In the context of a relationship, the talent doesn't have to be something you are into. The talent just has to be something that she can build a life around, outside of her mate. If you are not cultivating the talents you have, eventually you lose them. If you lose your talents, you lose a spiritual part of your personality. And to be frank, you become down right boring. It's upsetting to be in a room with your "gal" and you try to spark up an intelligent conversation and she can't bring anything to the table. You end up just watching TV or something. Conversation is a talent to me. To build on intelligent conversation, you have to be into current and past events and be able to articulate your interpretation of the world around you.

Like I said above, I do not want the relationship to be centered on me exclusively. I don't want all of the creativity and excitement to have to come from me. If I am busy, my mate should have something of her own interest that she can cultivate. I am not saying all I do is ME. I understand that time together is needed to keep the bond strong in a relationship. But what would make it extra special is to be able to be a part of and grow with each other's talents. I do not want to be in a situation like my mother. I love my mom to death, but in retrospect, her life was centered on my father and her sons' lives. She had talents with singing, craft work, martial arts and modeling. But during the duration of her relationship with my father, she never cultivated those talents and pretty much didn't do anything with them. My father and mother divorced when I was 13. I never heard them argue ONCE when I was young, so the divorce was a shock. They were married 12 years before the divorce. But now that I think about it, they never really conversed much or did things together. My dad was pretty much like me (into music, martial arts, etc.), so my mom was always at his concerts and Karate tournaments. Their life centered around him. Now if my mom would have cultivated her talents, he could have in turn been into something she was in and who knows where the relationship would have gone. I think the relationship would have been better if both of them were building each other up and supporting each other's endeavors.

When it all boils down to it, you don't want anything in the relationship to happen after a long period of time, only to realize that you never did any of the things your heart desired within the duration of that relationship. You don't want to come out feeling like you wasted your time. The cultivation of talents allows you to build a life outside of the relationship. The cultivation of talent in a relationship is not some shallow requirement for togetherness; it is something that keeps the relationship alive. It keeps the interest of each other alive. A man is proud of his woman who is successful with something she loves and has a talent for. Sometimes I am just attracted to a woman simply for the fact that she has the desire or is doing something with her talents. Talent is sexy. It forces you to think of someone in a whole new spiritual light.

So if you are a woman and feel you don't have a talent for something, STOP READING THIS ARTICLE NOW AND GO DEVELOP ONE! You will have a much more fulfilling life if you do. And if you are a woman

with talent and aren't afraid to use it, and are single, then give me a call at
....

He Pushed Me First

Tep, why are you in my office again? Every time I see you, you always fighting!

Principal Note Pad, and I know you don't like me to curse, but it wasn't my fault this time, it was the pen—that mutha phucka pushed me first!

There I was, minding my own business, composing forbidden scriptures using cutout Arabic alphabetic pictures, when suddenly this black ball-point pen came up to me talking shit. He told me to give him my mic because I didn't deserve it. Now see, I'm from the hood and you gosta protect yo stuff. I ain't no punk so I called this cat's bluff.

By this time, I am on my feet ready for something to pop off. I had my lyrical fist balled up, ready to knock his top off. There was no ending to this cat's yapping. I said, "Forget all this nonsense and let's starsta scrapping!" But before I could finish my sentence, this mutha phucka pushed me! I said to myself, "No this nicca didn't just push me!"

So I pushed the pen back. My mama taught me that you are a man and you don't take none of that. By this time a crowd had assembled. I ain't gonna lie, this was a big ass pen, so my heart began to tremble. The pen was talking noise and wouldn't shut up. He talking bout my poetry doesn't flow well and isn't witty enough. He talking bout my vocabulary is limited and my subject range is narrow. I need to go study more and make sure that the essence comes from the bone marrow.

I'm like are you crazy? I been breaking down unified field theorems since I was a baby. I studied the astronomical movement of the stars. I have conducted field research of what gas and mineral elements are contained on Mars. I've written dissertations in German and Cuneiform. I have in my personal collection the only living Hobits and unicorns. I've done two missions in Desert Storm and went for the hell of it to Vietnam. Because the Prophet Muhammad couldn't read or write, I helped him compose the Koran. I've calculated jet engine fuel fluctuations and carbon dated Austropolithicus bones beyond the first Wurm Period Glaciation. I've studied medicine and have performed various disease inoculations. I build software for super computers as a hobby, not as a working occupation.

So I started throwing dangling participles to see if he could take it. But I kept missing cuz he would lean back with his arms waving like the agent in the Matrix. So he threw six point Chinese stars of David. But I blocked it with a lightening bolt like on Street Fighter—just call me Lord Raden. He had a mean kick and I saw him aiming for my crotch. So I halted his move with a pressure point blow and gave him writer's block. So we retreat back into our preposition—both catching our breaths and reloading our ammunition. By this time the crowd is in a roar. The teachers in the hallway yell "stop" while the kids yell "encore."

We rev up for one last round. He been talking shyt for the longest and now it's time to throw down. I jump up in the air and take aim. The scene did a full 360 panoramic like the Matrix freeze frame. I give a HAAY-OOKID! The pen fell to the ground and he became weaker than an old woman with lupus. I heard a voice from the heavens say, "Finish him!" But that's when the school cops came and grabbed me by my limbs. Now I'm in your office giving explanations while the pen is visiting the nurse. But it wasn't my fault Principal Note Pad, it was the pen, that mutha phucka pushed me first!

If You're Still Not Convinced

There are cats in the poetry world who try their hardest to
     circumvent
The fact I left many stages ablaze, and they still not convinced
Second guessing my ability to turn mere words into prison contraband
Or my ability to create mathematical formulas
     Einstein couldn't comprehend
I can't help it if I am a Spoken Word embellisher
For safety measures, my pen comes complete with its own fire extinguisher
To extinguish the four alarm blaze left by my syntactical endurance
Before I spit at venues, my mics has to be covered by insurance
So the club won't be liable for the audience passing out
     from heat exhaustion
Cops arrest my poetry after the show and charge them mo flo's with arson
Please beg my pardon if I seem a little conceited
It's just that my poetry can walk on water
     and give sight to the blind like Jesus
Can make those walk who were once quadriplegic
Can humble the hearts of those who were once facetious
I've been known to tear down confidence
On Showtime at the Apollo I get on stage and boo the audience
I'm a super poet and only have one arch enemy
On a daily basis, I have to battle my own pen for word supremacy
I DJ with Saturn rings and use Uranus mountains to cross-fade
I plug my amp into the sun and illuminate space dust with ultraviolet rays
Aliens travel to my shows through the Milky Way
     like the New Jersey Turnpike
I wave my hands back and forth in front of the sun
     to give an illusion of a strobe light

I travel trough zodiac houses using celestial subways, trains and cabs
I hop in and out of galaxies like Bobby and Whitney out of rehab
I wash with natural moon soap while taking long meteor showers
And dry off naturally using the force of solar wind power
Poets cringe like when oxygen doesn't hit mitochondrial cells
    and they go into a lactate fermentation
I run the bottom of ocean floors like I'm moon-walking with
    my mouth open eating phytoplankton
While sea urchins ride ocean currents waving at other crustaceans
I'm moving tectonic plates causing earthquakes
    and other cataclysmic devastations
My poetic seismic meter registers *1906* off the Richter scale
My poetry is so sexy, it works as a stripper at Chip n Dales
If you're still not convinced as to who I am and what can I do?
If you're still pondering who I am and what can I do?

    I can build pyramids without the use of slave labor
I go through stages from vapor, solid, liquid and back to vapor
I can make a verb predicate to a noun
My poetry is so hot that when I sweat it dissipates
    and turns into cumulus clouds
I swallow hurricane water and spit over deserts to form an oasis
I make the Ku Klux Klan say, "Damn that nicca racist!"
I can make long distance phone calls using only my mental telepathy
My electromagnetic field span knocks Sirius B off its elliptical trajectory
And if you think that you can step to me
    or think that I can't spit spoken word
You better play like a penis in ya ear and phuck what you heard
You know it's over when you hear the fat lady drumming
And just like a deaf woman giving me head, you can't hear me coming

Where Did I Come From?

Before Your Time Type Poem

Now I must start off and say that my aim is not to offend anyone
To ride on my high horse or demean anyone
My aim is not to cause ruckus or dissention within the poetry scene
But only a few cats listening will understand what I mean when I say
I know **YOU** don't know nuttin bout this poem
cuz this poem is a before your time type poem

This poem was written when they used to play slow jams at the party
    type poem
When you came to the party to show off your latest routine type poem
This is a 77, 65, 44 and #2 bus route type poem
A "Hush your mouth before I give you something to cry about"
    type poem
This is a What's Happening Now, That's My Mama, Goodtimes
    type poem
This is a Sesame Street, Reading Rainbow, 321 Contact type poem
This is a "If you was really real type poem you'd remember Less than
    Zero, Burger Pattern by the Fatboys and Math-Net on Square One"
    type poem
This is a you wanted to go to a black college cuz of the cast of a
    Different World type poem
A time when you would lock yourself in your room with your WWF action
    figures with the kung fu grip and be in your own little world type poem!
This is a on Stage 3 of Super Mario Bros., hop on the turtle shell a dozen
    times to get 100 men type poem
This is about 20 people conversing on three-way type poem
This is a Bart Simpson pattern, Bobby Brown, Gumby hairstyle type poem
A Kwame, polka-dot, Hammer pants type poem

This is a 3rd Bass, Red Head Kingpin, Big Daddy Kane, Native Tongues,
    Flava Unit, BDP type poem
This is a Word Up, Fresh, Cold Chillin, Body Rock type poem

I know **YOU** don't know nuttin bout this poem
Cuz this poem is a before your time type poem

This poem was written when families ate together at the dinner table
    type poem
A time when dessert was served after that dinner type poem
This is a "My hair is like this cuz I got a little Indian in my family"
    type poem
This is a Jefferson's, Married With Children, All in the Family
    type poem
This is a every time Michael Jackson came out with a new video the world
    would stop to watch the premiere type poem
A Thriller jacket, shiny sock and glove, with the British Knights type poem
This is a Cross Color, Karl Kani, Marithe Francis Girbaud type poem
A one pants leg up, cap tilted back with head phones and back-pack to
        match type poem
This is a sugar water, peanut butter and syrup, dry cereal out the box
    type poem
This is a "Who the hell dun drunk up all the Kool-Aid?"
    denying it with your life type poem
This poem was written when everyone on your block could give you a
        whoopin type poem
A time when weave wasn't in style type poem
This is a Black and Old Gold, Ice Cold, Alpha runs the yard type poem
This is a …..

"Out of the night that covers me
Black as the pit from pole to pole
I thank whatever Gods may be
For my unconquerable soul"
type poem

This is a up up down down left right left right B A select start
　　　type poem
This is a kiss my Converse, who's the master, will teach me some *mooooves*,
　　Last Dragon type poem
This is a "You got that glow" type poem
A "Thunder, thunder, thunder cats, HOOOOOOOOO!" type poem
This is a Bam Bam Bigalo, Cocoa Beware, Jack The Snake type poem
A Hulk Hogan, Zeus, Andre The Giant, Ravishing Rick Rude type poem
This is a "Ha ha ha hum—You killed my brother—ha ha hum" type poem
This is a hug and kiss your girl cuz you love her type poem

Lord knows that **YOU** don't know nuttin bout this poem
Cuz this poem is a before your time type poem

Spirit And Spirituality: Another Way Of Saying Energy And How It Works

Introduction

At some period in time, most humans have contemplated what is the nature of spirit or the soul. Many seek answers through the guidance of a particular religious system and others seek answers through the workings of nature. I happen to have fallen into both categories during my life.

This inquiry into the nature of spirit naturally leads one along a path of wanting to understand spirituality. What is spirit? What is spirituality? What religious system has the answer? What is the process necessary for spiritual realization?

In my life's pursuit to answer these questions, I've come up with my own theories as to the nature of spirit and what spirituality really is. After an in-depth study into quantum mechanics, I've begun to look at the world a little differently and go against conventional orthodoxies when dealing with spirit and the so-called "spiritual world."

As I reflected on the many creation stories and the nature of energy, I've come to realize that science and religion were speaking about the same concepts, but in a different language. My current understanding of what spirit essentially is, is simply another way of saying energy. This essay attempts to connect the concepts of spirit and energy and how spirituality is simply a form of energy in use for a specified goal.

What is Spirit?

The orthodox definition of spirit, as per princeton.net, is:

• the vital principle or animating force within living things.
• the general atmosphere of a place or situation and the effect that it has on people; "the feel of the city excited him"; "a clergyman improved the tone of the meeting"; "it had the smell of treason."
• a fundamental emotional and activating principle determining one's character.
• any incorporeal supernatural being that can become visible (or audible) to human beings.
• emotional state: the state of a person's emotions (especially with regard to pleasure or dejection); "his emotional state depended on her opinion"; "he was in good spirits"; "his spirit rose."
• intent: the intended meaning of a communication.
• liveliness: animation and energy in action or expression; "it was a heavy play and the actors tried in vain to give life to it."
• heart: an inclination or tendency of a certain kind; "he had a change of heart."
• infuse with spirit; "The company spirited him up."

wordnet.princeton.edu/perl/webwn

In other words, spirit is the very animating substance of all living things. Spirit comes from the Latin root *spiritus*, meaning "breath." Breathing has been the ultimate symbol for life and thus its etymology.

There is another concept in nature that is the essence of all things and that is energy. Energy is the ability to do work, is what causes change or is the work that a certain force (gravitational, electromagnetic, etc.) can do. It, like spirit, is the animating force of all things in nature. Energy mainly takes on two forms: potential and kinetic, with other variations of the two (chemical, heat, nuclear, electromagnetic, and rest).

Potential energy is simply the energy that is present based upon an object's physical location within a given physical space. Kinetic energy is the energy an object possesses as a result of its motion. It is the work needed to accelerate an object from rest to its current velocity.

Spirit in essence is consciousness ready to be put to work. Spirit/energy has no form until it moves (See Quantum Mechanics and String Theory). Spirit and energy cannot be created nor destroyed; it can only change form. Energy is never at rest, it is always changing form (See Gabriel Oyibo and GAGUT). Although there is a thing called rest energy, which is energy when it is not moving relative to its inertial reference frame, this is only based on the appearance of a whole distinct object (as its smaller particles are always moving).

The soul then consists of individual pieces of spirit/energy that is conscious of itself as a distinct being. The soul in essence is the ID number for each spark of spirit matter. It is kind of like information that is on your computer. Information is stored on hard disks and assigned an ID number so when you need that information or a program to do tasks, it can easily be summoned to do what you want it to do. The ID number distinguishes this bit of "1's and 0's" from a different combination of "1's and 0's" that is bunched together on the magnetic disk. Imagine now these "1's and 0's" knowing they are "1's and 0's!"

I believe that spirit is man's potential and one of our many purposes in life is to carry out all of spirit's greatest possibilities through a process called spirituality. The human body is simply the vessel used to carry out tasks, just like your computer is simply the vessel, the mechanism, used to carry out various virtual tasks. The real essence (spirit) of the computer is the programs stored on the hard disks. The programs, combined with the creative faculties of the user, allow for all of the system's possibilities to be expressed in the context of completing various goals. This is how I see spirituality and I will further explain what I mean.

To recap for a moment, Spirit is another way of saying energy because they are both the animating essence of all living (and seemingly nonliving) things. Spirit and energy is the potential of all lifeforms waiting to be put to use and take form.

What is Spirituality?

Spirituality then is the actual potential energy of spirit being put to work. But I don't leave it there because there must be purpose and intent behind the work. Therefore, spirituality is the process of spirit realizing its full potential through the activities of service (kinetic energy), with the intent of enhancing the human condition. In order for one to be practicing spirituality, his/her energy must be exerted in activities that help the host (you) and others realize their full human potential.

Spirituality is an action word. It is not simply a frame of mind, something you read in a book or a set of rituals you perform. When you add the suffix "-ity" to a word, it means "state or quality of being." That means you are not potential (spirit/energy) anymore, you are actually in the state of that potential taking form; you are spirit fully expressed.

It is similar to when dark clouds have formed during a storm; the potential for there to be lightening and thunder is there because it has all of the components necessary for lightening and thunder. As soon as lightening occurs and it heats up the atmosphere, the air turns into plasma and expands and creates a sonic wave we call thunder. Not until there was some actual movement of the lightening (and all of the things that cause lightening) could there be actual thunder. It was a process of actual movement and it is the same with spirituality.

Misunderstood notions of spirituality

Oftentimes people relate spirituality with a specific set of dogma related to a particular religious system. I find this not to be the case at all. I view spirituality higher than religion, and for me, it is the second level of spiritual realization. Religion is for people just starting out on the journey. Unfortunately, people remain complacent at the religious level and never graduate beyond the myths and rituals that govern the system.

Religion is to be viewed as a stepping stone for self-realization and insight. It is the milk spoken of in the Biblical text. What you want is the meat and you can't get that on the first level (religion) on the path of spiritual realization (enlightenment). There is no one path to enlightenment. As each of us is born with a different set of fingerprints and personalities, our paths are as unique as the patterns that make up our fingerprints. It was easy in times past to believe in the one path dogma expressed by religious leaders: the majority of the population was illiterate and uneducated. But more and more people are coming to realize the personal aspect of spirituality because the majority of people can read now and are becoming educated on historical matters.

People get a new sense of what it means to be human and the possibilities of higher consciousness when they are involved in activities that enhance the human condition. The people who are not as spiritual are those who only do things for self-gratification. If it doesn't satisfy their bottom line, then they are not with it. The bottom line could be money, pride, or recognition for their works. Until their potential is expressed through service, they are not being spiritual.

How can one be more spiritual?

Spirit is essentially the stored potential of humankind, which has not realized (through service) its full potential. Spirituality is the kinetic movement of that animating energy towards realization of its potential through service which enhances the human condition. So to be more "spiritual" one must engage in activities that enhance the social, economic, physiological and psychological states of the people you interact with.

How is one able to realize those goals? In my opinion, one cannot begin the process of spirituality until one can answer for themselves, and can facilitate the process for others to answer for themselves, the following questions:

- Who am I?
- Where did I come from?
- What is my purpose?
- What must I do to fulfill that purpose?

The above questions have been the foundation of my spiritual journey (and essentially were the questions asked by our ancient ancestors who spawned all of the religious systems we practice today). But I often ask myself, "Is that all there is to it?" What comes after that? During one of my private periods of reflection, I came to the realization that there is more. Answering the questions above only allowed me to identify what the potential was for me. With this new perception of what spirit and spirituality is, I needed a guide for the realization of spirit's potential.

The second level of spiritual realization materializes when one is able to supply answers to these fundamental questions:

- What is the current condition of the world?
- What must be done to enhance the current conditions?
- What can I do with my talents and insight to improve these conditions?

• What methodologies and institutions must be in place to sustain these goals once realized?

At this stage it is no longer just about me, but I have inserted humanity into the equation. Selfless service to others is the basis of spirituality. Serving humanity allows the spirit to receive feedback. This is why this realm of existence was created (The Matrix): it is riddled with various sender and receiver objects that allow for perception in the midst of feedback. In order for spirit to "grow," it must do things (motion, kinetic energy, spirituality) that allow the controller, in a control system (the universe), to react and send feedback to the controller (spirit).

Memory is a necessary component, not only for survival, but for spiritual growth. Certain events in our lives stand out for the purpose of adaptation to external perturbations. But memory also serves as a mechanism, a kind of time stamp, for the purpose of personal reflection. Reflection is a major aspect of spirituality. This is why you have memories so you can go back and reflect and give meaning to events that have occurred so the spirit can grow and be one step closer to full realization of its potential (enlightenment). The chain of events is as so:

• The spirit has a set goal for improving the human condition.
• The spirit now puts in work and becomes kinetic energy (putting certain processes in place for spiritual realization).
• The event, once completed, has a certain affect on the soul and leaves an impression.
• This leaves a time stamp in the consciousness of the soul.
• The soul thus reflects on its activities and assigns value and meaning to the event.

Through meditation on the feedback given from the situation, the spirit begins the process of coming into its full potential and creates other experiences to further reach that goal, with its new insight and advanced methods for achieving those goals.

The most spiritual people in history were all in the business of making the world a better place, often at the expense of their own comfort and often their own lives. When I think of Malcolm X, Dr. Martin Luther King Jr., The Honorable Marcus Garvey, Harriet Tubman, Nat Turner, Mahatma Gandhi,

Mother Teresa, Urser Maat Ra Setep Em Ra (Ramesis II), Ayeshu (Yeshua, Jesus the Christ), Queen Ann Nzinga, Guatama Siddhartha, my (your) mother, and my (your) grandmother, I can't help but deify them because of the selfless service they have provided to humanity and their families. These are some of the greatest examples of spirituality personified.

One of my elders once told me:

> You just got to love Black people. Although sometimes they make you just want to give up, you have to keep going because the fight is bigger than Black people. A great leader is someone who understands that he/she may never see the fruits of his labor and he/she must persevere when no one tells them thank you.

Selfless service is at the heart of that quote.

What is the Matrix?

For those of you familiar with the popular film "The Matrix" (The Wachowski Brothers, 1999), you should be familiar with the question, "What is the Matrix?" The word Matrix means "womb." This is a very philosophical concept and gives us great insight to the nature and purpose of spirit.

Taking a cue from nature, we know that a woman's womb is where a new life is incubated for the purpose of developing (condensing spirit) into a full human being. Through this nine month period, all kinds of processes take place so that the lifeform's potential is realized and takes form within the womb. Once the physical processes have been completed, it is ready to be released onto the second part of its journey that we call life.

The universe works in the exact same way. The universe is a womb for spirits/souls and the physical world is the necessary location for this spiritual realization to take place. The universe creates the circumstances necessary to leave imprints on the consciousness, so the soul can reflect on the events, give meaning to the events, and grow so it can develop and prepare for the next plane of existence.

We tend to look at spirits as some separate, ethereal substance outside of the physical body. I propose that spirit and the physical body are the same thing. We can say that spirit and energy are the same, with the advent of Quantum Mechanics and the Newtonian Theory, because energy and matter are the same. There is no difference between matter and energy; they are just different forms of each other. The discussion on objects being another form of energy is beyond the scope of this essay, so I leave it up to you to study it on your own.

So in other words, the universe is the "spiritual realm." There is no separate realm outside of what is contained in the universe, for energy cannot be created nor destroyed, it can only change form. In order for it to change form, it must have form to begin with. Just because our five senses or the instruments we've created to enhance those senses cannot detect the most subtle form of energy, doesn't mean that the concepts exist outside of this reality.

The goal of spirituality is to experience the underlying consciousness that pervades the universe. The spirit cannot do this in its initial state of potentiality because knowledge can only be obtained through experience. Potentiality does not have sensory receptors to receive and send feedback to the initial consciousness. This is why spirit energy has to condense itself into matter and have experiences. The meaning of life could simply be to express all human possibilities and keep the ebb and flow of life going (since energy cannot be created nor destroyed).

The Matrix is a necessary construct so the soul can learn from the process of doing. You can't experience anything unless you have a location to experience it. The amount of energy put into having meaningful experiences is reflected in the spiritual maturity of the individual. One becomes spiritually mature when one is engaged in activities that enhance the human condition.

We have enough religion in the world; not enough spirituality (people in the business of righting the world's wrongs). Don't be satisfied just knowing what you are capable of, become kinetic energy and express all of the higher aspects of your potential. Pick a cause and dedicate yourself to the realization of its goals. Use your talents and insight to help further those goals. Imagine a world where the majority of people were consciously working to enhance the human condition. The Law of Attraction makes this a possibility (The Law of Attraction is a whole "nuva" discussion). With this frame of thought and belief in one's own capabilities, we'd have a more spiritual grounding and less dogmatic religions causing drama on the world stage. I hope this essay has given you enough so you can expand the discussion.

Lecture Notes: Jabade Powell

On Saturday, October 29, 2005, MOCHA Urban Hang Suite brought speaker Baba Jabade Powell with the Ta-Seti African Historical Society to Houston to speak on "Nile Valley Spirituality and its Step Children: African Influence on the Applied and Theoretical Sciences." It was a very informative lecture on the nature of African philosophy and science and how it later influenced the theoretical sciences of Europe. I take notes at lectures and I go home and do some research to see if the speaker's information is sound. After some research into the plausibility of the information, I like to summarize what I have learned. This article is really just my notes of some of the major aspects of the lecture. It does not include all of the information mentioned, but enough to where those who were not able to attend could get a gist of what was presented. My notes are as follows:

Theory of Special Relativity and Space-Time

The Theory of Special Relativity was coined by scientist Albert Einstein in a 1905 paper titled "On the Electrodynamics of Moving Bodies." This theory states that observers in an inertial reference frame, which are in uniform motion relative to one another, cannot perform any experiment to determine which one of them is in "absolute motion." The theory postulates that the speed of light would be the same for both observers. In other words, no matter where the observers are located and how they perceive the event, the laws of the universe are going to be the same regardless.

This theory by Einstein later prompted Hermann Minkowski to treat the three dimensions of space (height, width, length) and the one dimension of time as a single construct called the "Space-Time Continuum." This made space and time inseparable aspects of our reality. The theory of relativity posits that perception of an event is relative to your coordinates (location/space) and time of observation of that event. A social example would posit that how you see the world is based on the time in which you are living and the particular location or culture you belong to. Two people observing the same event, oftentimes view those events differently because they are viewing it from two different perspectives (locations) based on their upbringing and frame of reference. Any man or woman in a serious relationship can attest to this fact.

Well, this concept of relativity and space-time was already talked about and understood in ancient Ta-Merry (Egypt) 5,000 years before Einstein. All one has to do is take a look at the Mdw Ntr (hieroglyphic) writing and pay attention to the creation myths. The Mn-Nfr theology posits that the God Ptah (or Ta) rose out of the Nun (the ocean of consciousness of the creator). From this event, creation was able to happen. I am condensing this for sake of space, so forgive me. In Mdw Ntr, you can read words forwards and backwards and they all mean something different. The word / Ta / means to create or it could mean land. The word / Ta / in reverse is / At / and it means "moment." Here we have the fundamentals of space-time and relativity. Before creation can occur, you need a place to create—that would be / Ta / or Ptah rising out of the Nun. At the moment / Ta / (a place) was created, time was automatic (its reverse). In the physical realm, everything has an opposite. So the creation of Hot makes Cold automatic. The concept of Above makes the concept of Below automatic. One can't exist without the other, and so is the same with Space-Time. Before you can create anything, you need a place to put your creation. Time is the measure of two or more events. Creation is an event (including the place to create in) and creation happens in intervals called time. Here we see the Nile Valley people codifying science in myth 5,000 years before Einstein's Theory of Relativity and Minkowski's Space-Time Continuum.

Knum is what keeps us together

The ancient Ta-Merrians codified their scientific knowledge in myths. One myth talks about a Netcher by the name of Knum (Khunum, Chunum), who is often depicted fashioning man on his potter's wheel. He took the dust/clay of the earth and fashioned man from it. This should sound real "familiar" to persons of the Christian faith. If you haven't figured out by now, the "Gods" of Ta-Merri were not Gods in the sense that religious persons today would like to postulate. These Netchers were actually aspects of the one God personified for better understanding of that aspect of the creator. The ram headed deity Knum means union (and probably other things on other levels). Knum represents the element in nature called "sulfur." Sulfur was well known in ancient days, especially in the Biblical days. It was called "brimstone" in the Bible. Sulfur's colors are reddish gold or yellow, and when burned, it turns blue or violet.

Sulfur is essential to life. It is a minor constituent in fats, body fluids, amino acids and skeletal minerals. We get sulfur from plants that absorb the sulfate ion from the soil. This is one of the most crucial elements found in nature. Sulfur protects our cells from radiation and pollution. It helps to slow the aging process and prevents blood clots. More importantly, it keeps our skin elastic and supple. Without Sulfur, your body would just be the personification of the "Blob." From this you should be able to put together why "Knum" was responsible for "fashioning" man. Knum is the substance that gives us shape. This is just another example of how the ancient Kmtjw (Egyptians) codified their knowledge in the form of myth.

The importance of light

In the lecture we came across the symbol of a five point star that represents the goddess Aset (As, Isis). The name and symbols for Aset are many, so we will just focus on one aspect of this energy force. In this context the five point star used to represent her is to represent the five photons of light that human beings need to feel the sensation of sight. In one of her many myths it is said that "no mortal man has unveiled her" (Ashby, 81). One of her many attributes was love and the power to heal. Her son Heru (Hr, Horus) was bitten by a scorpion (one myth says a snake) and was near death. He was healed by the powers of his mother Aset. This particular myth deals with the healing power of light on the human body. This was a codified way of saying "photopheresis or extracorporeal photochemotherapy." Today this method is used to clean blood.

The treatment involves administering a drug called 8-METHOXYPSORALEN (8-MOP) that sensitizes cells to light. Then, some of the patient's blood is removed and the white cells in it are exposed to ultraviolent light and returned to the body. This procedure can inactivate some of the white blood cells that mediate the autoimmune reactions." - http://www.drweil.com/u/QA/QA98869/

Most, if not all, myths in Egypt have to do with mineral science, astronomy or health. In this particular case, we are dealing with health and how the power of light (Aset) can be used to treat toxins in the body. Full spectrum light has been used to treat behavior disorders such as ADD.

Conclusion

Needless to say, the Nile Valley occupants are not given the credit they deserve for introducing some of the major concepts in science and health to the world. I wish I could go into other things spoken about in the lecture including:

• Ta-Merrian introduction to the modern court system.
• The origins of the term technology.
• MAAT and the concept of law.
• General Systems Theory.
• The laws of thermodynamics.
• Everything flows – African origin of the Heraclites concept.
• Ahmes Papyrus and the computation of slopes for the building of the Pyramids.
• The periodic table and the 16 elements and Odu's of Ifa (and Modern Masonry with the Compass and Square).

We owe a great debt to Africa and I hope my notes and research has given inspiration for further research into the African contributions to world civilizations.

Web Resources:
http://www.wikipedia.com

On Sulfur
http://www.webelements.com/webelements/elements/text/S/key.html
http://en.wikipedia.org/wiki/Sulfur
http://www.mii.org/periodic/LifeElement.html

On Light
http://www.psych.utah.edu/~sc4002/psych3150/2Light.pdf
http://www.csulb.edu/~cwallis/482/visualsystem/eye.html
http://zoology.okstate.edu/zoolrc/biol1114/sampletests/previewmaterial/exam2/s01/prev-ex2S01.htm
http://www.scientificpsychic.com/workbook/chapter3.htm

Light used to treat diseases
http://www.alkalizeforhealth.net/ADHD.htm
http://www.findarticles.com/p/articles/mim0KWZ/is33/ai87703774
http://en.wikipedia.org/wiki/Chromotherapy
http://www.drweil.com/u/QA/QA98869/

On Aset
http://www.touregypt.net/godsofegypt/isis2.htm

Book References

Ashby M. (2000). *The Egyptian Book of the Dead: The Book of Coming Forth By Day.*. Florida: Cruzian Mystic Books
Cott J. (1994). *Isis and Osiris: A 5000 year old love story.*
    New York, New York:
    Double Day Dell Publishing, (tentative publication version)
Diop C. (1991). *Civilization or Barbarism: An Authentic Anthropology.*
    Brooklyn, New York: Lawrence Hill
Finch C. (2001). *A Star of Deep Beginnings: African Genesis of Technology.*
    Decatur, Georgia

African Societies Of Secret

Overview

African Societies of Secret are organizations whose primary role are to be the custodians and regulators for the harmonious functioning of a given community. These members help sustain and regulate the development of the ancient wisdom, traditions and culture of that group. The most distinguishing factor is their adherence to secrecy. Information regarding the collective wisdom is held secret by its members and is only revealed to those deemed worthy by elders, primarily during and after a rites of passage process.

The primary objective for keeping this body of knowledge secret is to protect its integrity and to keep it away from spiritually immature individuals who may use the knowledge for malicious purposes. This body of knowledge teaches its members how to govern society and maintain a balance between social groups. It also imparts knowledge of the universe and explains how to work the instruments of that society to manipulate its environment. This gives the group a competitive advantage over external or internal threats that may disrupt the balance of that society.

This body of wisdom has been passed down through ancestors who are believed to be accessible to those that know how to invoke and harness the energy through ritual. These ancestors have the information on how to draw on forces, powers and spirits for enhancing the quality of life here on Earth. The secrets on how to properly and successfully utilize these methods are held by qualified members of these groups.

While African Societies of Secret have many characteristics, the following three are the main identifiers: initiation rites, caste memberships, and the "sacred society"—the spiritual arm of the corporate group.

Initiation Rites

In many African societies, one is not an adult until one has completed an initiatory rites of passage process supervised by the elders of the community. Until they have completed a certain level of this process, they do not share in the privileges and duties of the community.

A Rite of Passage educates the youth in matters of marriage, procreation, sexual life and family responsibilities. This marks the beginning of acquiring knowledge, which is not accessible to them before their initiation. Neophytes are separated by gender and are taken away from the general corporate community. The goal is to develop latent physical skills, develop intellectual skills, endure hardships to alleviate the sense of fear of the unknown, learn to live communally, acquire specific vocational training and a healthy attitude toward honest labor, to learn respect for elders, and to learn the secrets of nature and the male/female relationship.

Initiation rites have many symbolic meanings. The ritualistic death and rebirth process signifies the dying to old habits and ways of thinking, living in the spirit world (thus being in isolation as in a woman's womb) and being reborn again into the corporate community. The initiate would then wear certain clothing and symbols that were not accessible to them before. They learn symbolic dances, handshakes and, in adult rites, a secret language only known to members of that group. For example, Dr. Gerhard Kubik discovered ideograms called Tusona (of a philosophic meaning) that are only known to the elders who speak the Luchazi language in the Kabompo district of Zambia. Initiates are often given new names after completion.

Initiation is not only for youth, as adults experience it several times throughout their adult life, usually until around age 72. A few African ethnic groups that practice such rites are the Yoruba of Nigeria, Akan of Ghana, and the Maasai and Akamba of Kenya.

Caste memberships

In many African societies one is born into a caste (not to be confused with hierarchal social castes such as in India, which mark them for life) or one may choose a caste when one chooses a career path. Castes are often associated with such professions as blacksmiths, iron smelters, stone masons, engineers, farmers and warriors. These castes are often apprenticeships in which initiates are taught the secrets of the craft, be it warfare or wood carving. An example would be the Dogon of Mali who have a caste for their "morticians." Although all castes are different, they all work for the betterment of the society.

Sacred Society

The Sacred Society deals with the spiritual component of a given society. The initiation rites and castes serve a spiritual component as well, but it is this aspect of the Secret Society in which we get our priests—people who are responsible for the upliftment of the soul. Many African priests use divination as a method to stay connected with spirit and to be able to draw upon spiritual energy to successfully complete mundane tasks for the society.

Many cultures in Africa use masks to tell stories of a moral character or, as in the case of the Dogon of Mali, use them to symbolically reenact the movement of the stars in a given constellation during open ceremonies. Only the duly initiated can wear certain masks.

There are many levels one can obtain in a priesthood in Africa. The Yoruba priests of Ifa, for instance, have different levels (three primarily) to their priesthood:

• Awo: first level initiate in the mysteries.
• Iyalorishas: mother of mysteries / Babalaworishas – father of mysteries.
• Oluwo: master of the mysteries (men exclusively).

Compare the above with the three levels known in the ancient Kemetic priesthood:

• Mortals: students who were being instructed on a probationary status, but had not experienced the inner vision—neophytes.
• Intelligences: students who had attained inner vision and had received a glimpse of cosmic consciousness.
• Sons of Light: students who had become identified with or united with the light (God)—masters of the mysteries.

Conclusion

African Societies of Secret serve as the vehicle that organizes and social-izes communities and families in a manner that uplifts the society and keeps it cohesive. It also serves as an educational medium through an initiation rites of passage for members at various stages in life. The higher knowledge held sacred by elders is held secret to outsiders and is only revealed to mem-bers worthy to obtain it, usually in steps and phases. This insures the integri-ty of the body of wisdom against malicious use by individuals not mature enough to use it constructively. African secret societies are as old as time itself and serve as the very fabric that gives Africa its unique characteristics.

Further Readings:

Butt-Thompson, F.W. (2003). *West African Secret Societies*
Dieterlen G, Griaule M., (1986). *The Pale Fox*
Fu-Kia, K. Bunseki (2001). *African Cosmology of the Bantu-Congo: Principles of Life and Living*
James, G.M. (1954). *Stolen Legacy*
MBiti, J.S. (1970). *African Religions and Philosophy*

Interview:
Professor James Smalls

On February 26, 2005, professor James Smalls, now residing in New York city, visited the city of Houston to present a lecture, "Secret Societies: From the Nile Valley to West Africa." The Ta-Seti African Historical Society is responsible for bringing this subject to the forefront during African History Month and to the greater Houston area by sponsoring the event at the Shrine of the Black Madonna museum on this date. The lecture was very informative. It brought to light and demystified the issues with African secret societies: their purpose and function within those societies. Many were not able to make it to the lecture and missed out on all of the great information given.

I wanted the MOCHA audience to catch a glimpse of the many issues discussed during this lecture by Mr. Smalls, or Baba Oba Joko Ade Byo as he is known in the Yoruba priesthood. I caught up with Baba Smalls at his hotel room as he was getting ready to board the plane headed back to New York. He agreed to meet with me briefly to reiterate some of the things expressed in the lecture for the greater MOCHA audience. We are glad he took the brief time to talk to us. The interview is as follows:

MUHS: What is a secret society and what does it consist of?

JS: A secret society is basically an organization of persons, of any community, whose primary role is to be the custodian of the wisdom that keeps that community functional, keeps that community together. And secrets are that body of information that people don't know or don't have general knowledge of or that the elders or the leaders of that community feel should not be imparted to the general community except in steps and phases. And again, that's the educational system of any ethnic group that deals with the development and the protection and the sustaining of that ethnic group's ancient wisdom and traditions and culture.

MUHS: What are some of the myths associated with secret societies; that they're on some world domination or they have secrets to life in which they don't want to dispel to others?

JS: Well, I'm not that concerned with non-African secret societies, but when you talk about the myth of secret societies, you are basically talking about many of the European organizations, the Masons, Rosicrucians, Knights of Pythias and Odd Fellows, which now manifest itself in the Black community, along with the others, Illuminati. They're basically organizations dealing with the same body of knowledge, basically African body of knowledge. Most of them got the body on knowledge from Egypt via Greece or via the Christian Church during the Crusades. And the body of knowledge we are talking about is how to organize society, how to organize family, how to instruct and socialize your society so that it does what you want it to do. And many organizations used that, and especially in the West, to dominate other people. Ignorance leaves people weak. So if the information that would allow people to organize in a positive constructive way for their own survival is cut from them, then those that have the information become the dominate element in that society.

Now secret societies are not limited to any community. Every community in the world has secret societies. The primary reason is to protect and sustain the integrity of the body of knowledge that sustains the community and the ethnic groups and their cultures.

MUHS: How does one do a comparative of old secret societies which have been in existence for thousands of years unbroken and its (the model of ancient secret societies) functioning within the context of the United States of America with trying to build a community here? Or is that even possible using the methods of a secret society?

JS: First, you want to know too much. There are some things you shouldn't know, you have to earn the right to know. A secret society can be used anywhere. A secret society is a group of people who hold a secret. A secret is something that someone else doesn't know. And in secret societies for the most part, we are talking about a body of knowledge that teach you how to organize, sustain and maintain groups of people, interaction within society, the wisdom and the science of the universe, that shows you how to work your instruments of society so that it works to your advantage. It will work anywhere in the world. Japanese have secret societies. Chinese have secret societies. Indians have secret societies. Native Americans have secret societies. That has always been the place where the body of knowledge that sustain and promote a community are maintained and the integrity and honesty of that knowledge is maintained. So we can use it anywhere in the world. But it must come from a place of integrity. It must come from a place built on morality and honesty and principles that grow people and not demean people.

MUHS: Many people feel that so-called secret societies should be more open, that they should function more so like an NAACP or something. What is your opinion on that?

JS: It's a silly point of view and anybody who holds that conception has nothing to do with secret societies. If it was open it wouldn't be a secret anymore now would it? So no, you have to have a way to protect the integrity of the knowledge of ancestors so you can use it for the advantage and the development of your people. That's the primary thing. The NAACP is a social organization and political organization designed by "White" folks to use "Black" folks as cannon fire to change laws in this country... that was the advantage of Jews and Irish minorities without the Blacks having any sustainable victories and [they] have been very successful.

MUHS: I have a book in my hand, "Isis and Osiris" by Jonathan Cott. This is the unpublished version and it's Eurocentric in its perception. They are following so-called Ammonite (secret society of Europeans in Egypt) and I want to read from the work (page 124-125). Something you said in your lecture last night reminded me of this and I wanted to get your opinion of this. Basically what it says is this:

Tie   Ammonite   Foundation Pg. 125

"Whether or not Ausar and Auset are thought of as real or mythological," I said, "How do the Ammonites think of these two racially? Are they thought of as black or brown or white?"
"There are some books that say that Ausar was white and that he came

into Egypt from Libya. Auset, on the other hand, came from the East, and she was yellow. This convergence was here in Africa where the majority of the people are black. In the Nile Valley, during early times, there was every color of people. Some of us were white, some brown, some a kind of yellow color, some Black. It depended on what part of the tribe you were from. And we have direct relation to the Dogon people in Mali. They tell the story that they went to the south and we went to the north, and that we will one day reunite. They call us the People of the shining Faces and Those Who Write upon the Mountains with fire. Also, there were a few Pharaohs who were black. There was no discrimination based on color here. We're all Nilotic people, and no race is exalted above another.

"But the Ammonites believe that you should marry within the faith and someone of your own genetic background and your own racial background: Rh-negative marries Rh-negative; Rh-positive, Rh-positive; brown marries brown; white, white; black, black. We see that God created every race for a purpose. There's a part of our writings that asserts that Auset created the brown people, Sekhmet Montu created the yellow people, Ra created the white people, and Heru created the black people. The writings also state that the blacks will be the salvation of humankind— the freeing of the black people will be the freeing of earth from the bonds of negativity and materialism—and that the Book will be given to all people when the black people are free. So if we can bring all of the colors of the Earth into equality and bring forth the Hope, which is the black people, because Heru was black in his form of eternity, then the whole world will manifest the Holy Family."

JS: Is this person Black or White?

MUHS: White

JS: And he speaks like a White man. Most of that are lies, misconceptions and White folks tripping. And I usually don't deal with White folks tripping over crap. How would Black folks let a Yellow person come from one way…White person come from…that's bullshit. The Libyans were as Black as the other Africans. And it's clear about color. We were dealing with color as far back as the 8th century. 8th century Iraq you have Jahiz (Abu-Uthman

Amr ben Bahr Al-Jahiz) writing books like *The Superiority in Glory of the Black Race Over The White*. That was in the 8th century AD. I got a copy of his book. Most White folks got their knowledge of Isis and Asar/Aset from the Greek writing. As the Greeks tried to "whiten" up that society, which they conquered parts, much of what he just said is myths, misconceptions and White folks dreaming.

There was no such thing as "a few pharaohs were Black"; all of the legitimate pharaohs were Black. Those that came in during the invasions of the Greeks, Persians and Romans, they weren't pharaohs. They were crackers who tried to usurp and dominate and colonize and imperialize our society. We do not consider them as legitimate; they were not our leaders. We did not choose them; they did not come from the bloodline. A pharaoh comes from a particular bloodline that goes back thousands of years. That's how you are chosen. You cannot be the leader just being smart. You had to come from a particular gene pool, and that gene pool had a lineage and an antiquity that was part of the founding family that was part of the very first dynasty, and they were Black folks and they still are Black folks.

MUHS: Well, I thank you so much for, and I am humble in your presence, for taking the time to interview with us. Is there anything in particular that you would like to say in closing, in relation to the topic at hand?

JS: Yes, Black folks just need to stop being afraid to be Black folks. They go to church and they worship their God and they say they believe in God and truth and believe that God don't make no mistakes. God made us first, God made us Black. Now if you are down with your God, whether it's Allah, Jehovah, Jesus, or Yahweh, either your God is a liar and you really don't believe in him, but if you believe in him, then God made us perfection in Black. We know that Black folks are the mother and father of everybody else on the planet Earth. Start acting like it. And that makes God your primary ancestor. Start acting like you're God having a human experience and stop being afraid and stop punking up. Because your love for White people is so deep, you want to pretend that you're ignorant of Black facts, so you can continue to make love to this homosexual freak that rules the world. Get it right, be Black, get back in your place.

Black People Suffer From Short-term Memory

I see we forget
Oh how soon do we forget?
The struggles
The heartache
The time that was spent
Fighting
And dying
For we neglect our history
Oh how we suffer from short-term memory

In this Age of Aquarius, where knowledge is abound
We graduate top of our class
But knowledge of self can't be found
We've gained material things
But our souls have been depleted
If you don't know your history
You'll be doomed to repeat it

I came up with this topic
After deep contemplation
The most compelling situation is when we talk about reparations
When the Japanese and Indian and Jews yell reparations
With no hesitation
We champion their cause
But when Blacks yell Repair our Nation
We dismiss it just because
They told us you don't need reparations

Slavery was so long ago
Blacks are doing well now
Look at the rappers in the videos
You guys are coming up now
You should all be so proud
You're even infiltrating the government
Just look at Collin Powell

But I don't take it to heart
Because I know it's all for show
How did we have more businesses in the midst of Jim Crow?
What happened to our hotels and banks and hospital floors?
Our cleaners and barbers and grocery stores?
Our leaders, our music, our culture, our schools?
Now we're on TV straight acting like fools
When I think back to who we were
The feeling makes me sick
I begun to get depressed when I realize that Blacks don't make toothpicks
We must remember that we're great and we'll always be great
But God can't help you if half-way you won't meet
A people without a historical consciousness isn't fit to be free
Oh how we suffer from short-term memory

When we get a little change
Our personalities begin to change
No longer can we associate ourselves with the ghetto and thangs
No longer do we have an ear
Or time to volunteer
It's all about me now so step to the rear
I've gotten where I am because I laced my boot straps
I needed no help, I put myself on the map

So who is a counselor?
A pastor
A prayer
A scholarship
A hook-up
A family that cares
I got here because of my talent, my drive and my wit

Oh Black people, how soon do we forget?

We are in the condition we're in
Because we're programmed to forget
We fail to realize all of the time that was spent
Marching in protest for our human rights
In this day and age and we still can't unite
We digest everything they feed us
From Black people can't get along to a Caucasian Jesus
We forget how valuable our neighborhood *is*
Until real estate companies yell out their first bids
We gave respect to elders, cuz it was nothing less than proper
Before the 1960s, Blacks never visited the doctor
We cured various lacerations and sicknesses and burns
With the aid of some prayer and some ointment and herbs
We united countries together with the sound of our hymns
But all rappers profess is their new shiny rims
We were the pinnacle of health but that's back in the days
Now we're the number one ethnic group most infected by AIDS

I see we forget
Oh how soon do we forget?
The struggles
The heartache
The time that was spent
Fighting
And dying
For we neglect our history
Oh how we suffer from short-term memory

But you see, I still remember
I said all is not lost because
I still remember
I remember a time when....
We built great architectures
Europeans used to travel for miles just to hear one of our lectures
I remember when all of our food was home grown
We couldn't afford cameras
So we chiseled our face in stone
When there wasn't enough water to support our civilization

We simply channeled river water and invented irrigation
When enemies invaded, we were prepared for their arrival
We hid our knowledge in parables and called it the Bible
I remember a time when we didn't need locks
Car alarm, fences or neighborhood cops
A time when compassion and love was shown
And pride was felt when you supported Black-owned
When we could rock the bells and let freedom ring
When dancers could dance and singers could sing
I mean Sang
We were doing our thang
Everyone was creative and we went against the grain
We thought outside the box
We wore corn rolls and afros and braids and locks
When the church was the center for political organization
When individual thrust was for the good of the nation
When you were in trouble and a friend you could call
When our children was the reason we even struggled at all

I see we forget
Oh how soon do we forget?
The struggles
The heartache
The time that was spent
Fighting
And dying
For we neglect our history
Oh how we suffer from short-term memory

Writer's Block

With Black folks, it's all about representing
It's about representing your peoples
Representing where you come from

See, I live on writer's block
It's kinda down the street from *present*, but you have to go a little *past tense*
A little past Spanish Blvd.— you can tell by the *accents*
Where the illest word-smiths reside and it's home of the best emcees
Where you'll find cops and the thugs together smoking poet-trees
Inhaling fumes of burnt offerings prepared for the ancestors
Giving birth to poems, watching words grow every trimester

I remember a sista named Stacy and damn was she fine
She used to have this boyfriend by the name of "mine"
He was a very *possessive pronoun* and he used to mistreat her
He used to beat her outside next to the parking meters
She yearned for the day of her independence
She finally took him to court and now he's serving a 10 year *run-on sentence*
To understand what went wrong is really quiet simple
She used to give 100% in the relationship, while he only gave *participle*

There were a lot of lessons to be learned on writer's block
Like covering up during a brain storm
   and when debris starts flying you better jot
Down whatever comes to mind, cuz that's where the thoughts lurk
Like how we used to get in trouble for saying cursive words in church
In school we learned how to *sub-tracks* and *add-verbs*
We used to try our hardest to deflower and di-verg
Ons, and nerds were the worst ones
Because they say there's nothing new under the sun

So we look over the sun and wait for inspiration to come
So we can unite with the gods like words do in conjunctions
I was broke den a mug, and didn't have money for the life of me
I remember sneaking into the movies because we
  couldn't afford the *apostro-fee*
I remember my first concert as a teen watching Cameo
It was at the Microsoft Word-up theatre, live and in stereo
On writer's block, we don't run our mouths, we run our minds
We run-on sentences and jump subjects from behind
All elders on the block are word-priests
  and have magic spells to turn mics into gold
Haiku or prose –
We spit freestyles until the sun goes
Down
Until Berlin walls come
Down
It's a low *down*, dirty shame how rich poets
Want to come on writer's block
Planning regentrification of the craft, while real poets
  are being herded out like livestock
Making the bullshyt level so high that real poets can't afford to sacrifice
  any more brain cells, so they don't come back
Where open mics become open forums for new comers
  to spit pussy poems that's whack
But on my writer's block, we nah havin nat, ras clot, bombaclot bull-shyaht
We resurrect biggie and Tupac, playing nothing but underground Hip Hop
On top of roof tops, were people don't dread their locks
Where we make plans to build imagi-nations and freedom declarations
Where spoken word is a respected occupation
  and there's no need for disease inoculations
Until the mother ship creates one nation, under a groove
I'll be under a lamp writing poetry, listening to Dwele sho improve
That's how we do it on writer's block

What Is My
Purpose?

Enter The
Seven Chambers Of Poetry

Introduction

Poetry is an artistic form of self-expression that has allowed human beings to bring meaning to various human experiences long before written records. As a poet, I often look for ways to better convey messages that will impact an audience in the most positive way. Few poets have the ability to capture an experience and are able to relay that experience with meaning and practicality, while at the same time being creative and entertaining. These are your master poets.

These master poets have a way of taking seemingly unrelated topics and weaving the concepts into a new perspective in a manner in which only a poet can do. In my quest for a more integral approach to poetry, I sought out a process that would help me to reach that final level of mastery. How would I need to write? What do I need to study? What must I eat? Who should I study? What should I talk about? What should I do to enhance myself as a person as well as an artist?

The answer came to me one day while viewing one of my favorite all time martial arts films: *36 Chambers of Shaolin*. I've always believed that the spirit of martial arts and the spirit of poetry were one and the same, but I was never able to articulate the connection. After watching the film recently it suddenly came to me. Just like with the ancient African mysteries systems, learning and development comes in degrees. One must master a particular aspect of self before moving on to the next level.

This was the sentiment so eloquently expressed in the film. Like the Shaolin monks of the Shaolin Temple, in order for poets to master the art (and ultimately master themselves), a poet must master each chamber of poetry to become that master poet. So I came up with Seven Chambers of

Poetry that, in my opinion, must be mastered in order to become a great artist.

The 35 Chambers of Shaolin

The Shaolin temple was established in China in 495 AD during the Wei Dynasty (386-534 AD). It was created to initially house an Indian priest named Batuo who came to Luoyang, the then capital of China, to spread the teachings of Buddhism. The emperor Xiaowen was a believer in Buddhism and had the temple built in the Songshan mountains so Batuo could teach the philosophy.

Bodhidarma, a famous Buddhist monk, came from India to China in 517 AD. He was the creator of Chinese Zen and is rumored to be the founder of Chinese martial arts. He created the 18 postures of Sho Pan Lo Han (18 Postures of Lohan) for the monks to learn for self-defense. The Shaolin temple has been the target for destruction for many years, so the monks were forced to learn how to defend it.

The Shaolin temple created a second order of fighter monks who were allowed to leave the temple and teach the teachings to bring recruits to the temple. This sect was called the "White Lotus Society" and was given permission to teach non-Buddhists the philosophy. As mentioned earlier, the many styles were developed as a result of centuries of having to defend themselves against invading armies. From this bit of history was born the 35 Chambers of Shaolin. The 35 Chambers of Shaolin are simply the degrees and forms that must be mastered within Shaolin Gongfu. There are approximately 35 pressure points within the human body and they are the focus of Pressure Point Fighting in the style of Dim Mak. Unity of the mind, body and spirit are the focus of the system. As an apprentice, you would have to master the following chambers:

NOVICE CHAMBER(s) (Life Begins)

Chamber 1—Green Sash (Spring)
a.) Lohan Salutation
b.) 6 Novice Stances
c.) 1st Standard of Shaolin
    Chamber 2—Blue Sash (Summer)
a.) 5 Novice Kicks
b.) 2nd Standard of Shaolin
    Chamber 3—Purple Sash (Fall / Autumn)
a.) 10 Novice Break-Fall and Training Techniques
b.) 3rd Standard of Shaolin

The Chakra System

Given the nature of the 35 Chambers of Shaolin and how they relate to pressure points in the body, I wanted my system to have a physiological reference as well. But I do not think you need 35 styles of poetry to be considered a master poet, so I reduced them to that oh so spiritual number seven and related it to the Chakra system. So before I go into the Seven Chambers of Poetry, I thought I'd introduce the Chakra system to those unfamiliar with it.

The word Chakra is Sanskrit for wheel or disk and signifies one of seven basic energy centers in the body. Each of these centers correlates to major nerve ganglia branching forth from the spinal column. In addition, the Chakras also correlate to levels of consciousness, archetypal elements, developmental stages of life, colors, sounds, body functions, and much, much more.

In brief, the seven chakras are as follows:

1. **Earth**: Physical Identity, oriented to self-preservation—the spine.
2. **Water**: Emotional Identity, oriented to self-gratification—abdomen, lower back, sexual organs.
3. **Fire**: Ego Identity, oriented to self-definition—solar plexus.
4. **Air:** Social Identity, oriented to self-acceptance—heart.
5. **Sound**: Creative Identity, oriented to self-expression—lungs.
6. **Light**: Archetypal Identity, oriented to self-reflection—brow or third eye.
7. **Thought**: Universal Identity, oriented to self-knowledge.

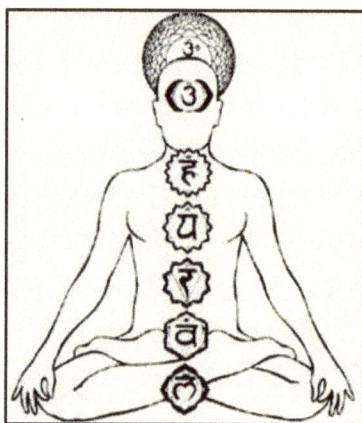

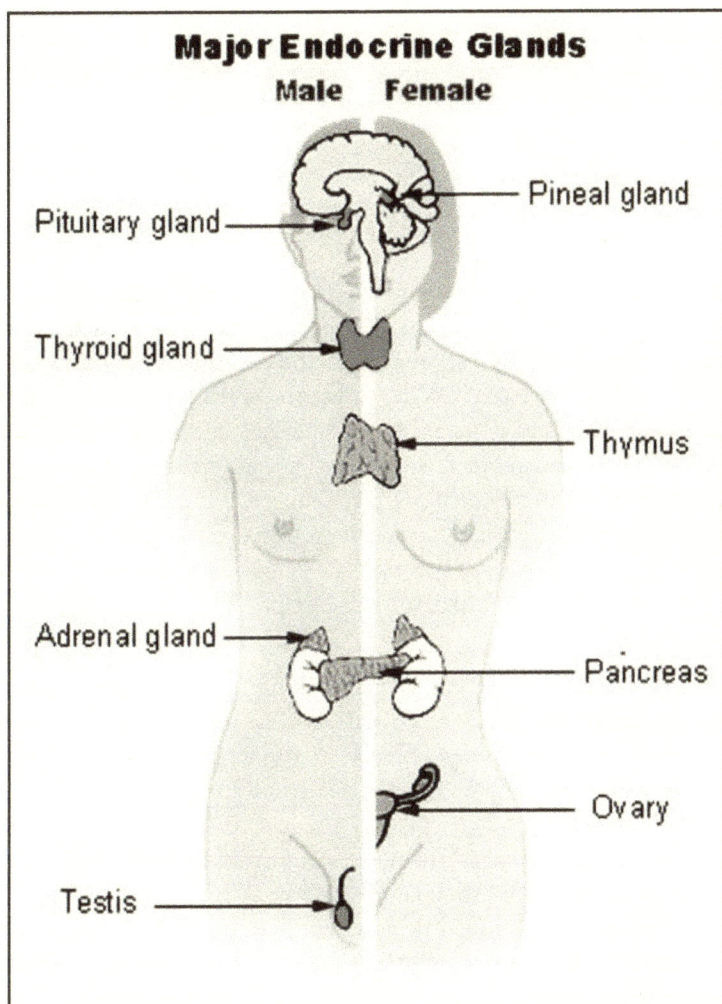

Major Endocrine Glands
Male Female

Pituitary gland

Pineal gland

Thyroid gland

Thymus

Adrenal gland

Pancreas

Ovary

Testis

The intricate details of the Chakra system will not be explored here as it is quite extensive and will bring us beyond the parameters of this particular discussion. I will leave that up to you to study in your own time. I will say, however, that the Chakra system is a system of human spiritual evolution and each Chakra represents a state of consciousness. Your life force energy (Kundalini) must go up these states to bring one to the last Chakra, the Crown Chakra, which ultimately is self-awareness, enlightenment, nirvana or Buddha.

Each Chakra represents vortices of energy. By understanding these psycho-spiritual centers and removing obstacles to them, Kundalini energy is freed and you are able to move toward the divine essence of your being. This is essentially how I relate the Seven Chambers of Poetry. So instead of saying Chakras, I will use Chambers.

The Seven Chambers of Poetry

After all of that information, it's now time for the bare bones of the philosophy. Each chamber is named after a concept or person in which I think represents or personifies the very nature of the chamber. Each chamber is an area that must be mastered in order to become a master poet. This list is not meant to be treated as dogma. I created it as a guide for poets who aim to go beyond the mundane in their writing and performance. I am a performance poet: I like to perform my pieces as I feel there is more energy given to poems when performed versus them being read on paper.

Chamber of Diop

I named the very first chamber after one of the greatest intellectuals of our time, Dr. Cheikh Anta Diop, from Senegal West Africa. He is considered the pharaoh of Africana studies because of the wealth of knowledge he brought to the discipline and because of his multi-disciplinary approach to history and social policy.

Dr. Diop was a physicist, linguist, historian, anthropologist, and Egyptologist, and he set the foundation for true Africological studies. His expertise in the above mentioned fields allowed him to put into perspective and reconstruct the true history of Africa and its inhabitants. Not only was he able to properly reconstruct our history, but with that knowledge he was able to formulate workable solutions to the many problems Africa faced at the time that could help to eliminate the social and economic conditions that plague the continent to this date.

A poet's job is to be able to take history and formulate new solutions to age-old problems. With this you need a solid foundation of historical events and a working knowledge of how the universe works around you. The study of the universe and its history gives a poet much to draw from when composing his or her solutions to modern day problems.

You can't be a great writer unless you are first a great reader. I can't stress enough the importance of reading to expand one's horizons and conscious level. It shows in your works and people can gain more from your insight because you are able to draw from various human experiences. I encourage you to read about history, religion, spirituality, meta-physics, philosophy, art, music, medicine, physics, the human anatomy, language and architecture.

Not only should the study of the world be the focus, but the study of the artform itself. What forms are there? Who are the poets who came before me? Why were these considered great? What did they talk about? What didn't they talk about? What must I do to stand out from these greats of times past? Only by answering these questions and more will you be able to gain a more holistic perspective of life and how best to articulate it.

This is related to the first Chakra of earth, in that it is your foundation. This is your grounding and you can't move up the energy centers until you have grasped this particular energy at the base of the spine. Just as the spine helps to shape the back, which is a major support system of the body, so will mastery of this chamber shape the nature of your work and perspective.

Chamber of Jeet Kune Do

Jeet Kune Do is a martial art form created by the great philosopher, actor and martial arts master Bruce Lee. Jeet Kune Do means "way of the intercepting fist." It was a philosophy developed by Lee in 1967 as a "style of no style," "using no way as a way." He was speaking about the flexibility of this martial art style as it is not confined to specific moves to accomplish the desired result.

Bruce Lee in an interview said, "Ultimately, martial art means honestly expressing yourself. It is easy for me to put on a show and be cocky so I can show you some really fancy movement. But to express oneself honestly, not lying to oneself, and to express myself honestly enough, that, my friend, is very hard to do."

He saw martial arts as a form of honest expression. Bruce Lee and I think of our passions in the same light. I also believe that poetry should have no form or set ways of expression. Limited styles bring limited perspectives and we can't grow as poets unless we are flexible.

This is why Jeet Kune Do was chosen for this chamber. This chamber coincides with the Chakra of water. Bruce Lee has been quoted as saying, "Be formless... shapeless like water. If you put water into a cup, it becomes the cup. You put water into a bottle, it becomes the bottle. You put it into a teapot, it becomes the teapot. Water can flow, and it can crash. Be water, my friend..."

This is the chamber of creative experimentation. After you have gained a substantial amount of knowledge about the universe, here is the chamber where you ultimately express it in written form. The objective is to create new ways of articulating the human experience. This is not a chamber to be restricted by form. This is your opportunity to break all of the rules and expand the poetic boundaries. Here you can write for the sake of writing. The aim is to push the poetic boundaries.

The sexual organs are used to create life on the physical plane. This is why it is used as the charka of creativity. Art and sex, to me, are the same. They are both just processes that put concepts to form. I am not like the church, I encourage you to have sex. Have sex with possibilities. Impregnate the subconscious and give birth to creative, thought provoking poetry.

Chamber of Ra

Ra is an Egyptian deity who represents the vital life force of creation. According to Egyptian myth, he is represented by the sun disk and is the creator of all life. This chamber is represented by the element of fire. Fire in this sense is equal to passion. Now we are going beyond being creative for the sake of being creative. Now we are writing with purpose and intent. Our intent is to write about issues that are passionate to us. There must be a type of energy felt in our writing at this stage.

This chamber is represented by the solar-plexus. When this chamber is mastered, it will give your poetry life. It will become more effective and will give your poetry power to inspire minds and provoke action.

Chamber of Simone

This chamber is named after the great pianist, vocalist, activist and song writer Nina Simone. This chamber represents the element of air. Her vocal style is characterized by passion and breathiness. When this chamber is mastered, it allows us to love deeply, feel compassion, and have a deep sense of peace and centeredness.

Nina Simone's talents spanned many genres: R&B, jazz, bebop, blues, gospel, folk and pop. Her style was not limited to any one genre, which makes it hard to characterize her music. Just like her talents, our talents shouldn't be limited to just writing poetry. Your talents should expand many different things so you can integrate all of your arts into a single creation all of your own.

Nina Simone was also an activist. She encouraged us to not only talk about issues, but to be living solutions. This is what must be done on this level. Reading is all fine and dandy, but if you aren't working to eradicate the very problems you're reading about, or enhance the very conditions you speak about in your work, then you are a poet without purpose.

Her music was passion felt. Her music provoked thought. Her music had meaning and purpose. Her music sustained life. Air is the most essential element our bodies need. Purpose and love are the most essential elements needed in poetry and this is why they are related to the heart Chakra. Nina Simone is legendary because she had all of the right elements and you can be too if you follow her lead.

Chamber of Ptah

Ptah is another Egyptian deity who is also responsible for creation, but he is unique because he is the first in recorded history to speak the world into existence (see Shabaka Stone). The Chamber of Ptah is the Chakra related to the lungs and sound. Quantum Mechanics has posited that ultimately the universe is made of waves called strings. It is believed that these strings respond in shape to various pitches of sound.

The poet has the same creative powers as Ptah. We can speak certain things into existence. At this level, we are in the realm of performance. Here you will be working on how best to project your voice and give life to your poem. The throat is responsible for creating the sounds that come out of our mouths. This is a good time to hit up as many open mic poetry spots as possible so you can practice speaking in front of a crowd.

This is the training ground for good performance poets. Here you can see if the audience hangs on your every word or can't wait for you to get off the stage. A good performance poet has a powerful voice and commands the attention of the audience. A powerful voice combined with well written poetry can be an invigorating experience for your audience members.

Being able to change your octaves can add emphasis to certain concepts or points during a performance. You don't want to be monotone and dull. Just like different frequencies of sound in nature produce different forms of matter, the different fluctuations in your voice create different feelings for your audience. You want them to experience different emotions and your mastery of sound and language can take them there. To evoke emotions in your audience is your goal. Emotions are vibratory experiences that cause us to move. You want your audience to move in a direction that leads them to a place that will help them to better understand themselves.

Chamber of MAAT

The goddess MAAT is another Egyptian deity. She also represents a profound philosophical concept. MAAT has several meanings and they include order, justice, reciprocity, righteousness, balance and harmony. Balance and order is what we seek in our spiritual lives, our communities and in our social atmosphere. MAAT regulates the movement of the universe. Without MAAT, there would be nothing but chaos and disorder.

While MAAT is more known for the aspects of order, balance and harmony, our focus in this chamber is her aspect of justice. The goddess MAAT is sometimes depicted with a blindfold or a veil covering her eyes. In the temples of Egypt, you will find depictions of the kings offering a figure of "blind" MAAT. It symbolizes the legitimacy of the ruler to aspire to divine consciousness. Most Egyptologists assume that the "blind" MAAT symbolizes objectivity and non-bias in judgment, as the king was the final judge of law. But this is farthest from the truth.

In order to judge or rule a nation one must be able to see. The blindfold was a reminder to the king of his responsibilities as a ruler. You don't want blind justice. You want justice that is based on clear and concise evidence that everyone can see. Sight is the most important thing to possess in order to judge.

As an artist, you must be able to see, not only with your physical eyes, but intuitively. Now we are getting into the spiritual aspects of the art form. In order to bring revelations to the people, you must be able to see beyond the mundacity, beyond the superficiality of what's apparent on the surface of events. The job of a poet is to be able to look at the code of the matrix and interpret the underlying meaning of a situation and present it to the people in a manner that will resonate in their subconscious.

This chamber is related to the Chakra of light. It is what we consider the "third eye." When mastered, you will be able to, in a sense, "see the big picture." Although you are in a higher stage of poetic development, here the challenge is still to present the information in a manner that is easily understood to a general populace. A person who has mastered this level of poetic writing can talk about the slave trade and relate it to humanity's social immaturity and how slavery is destined to happen again unless humanity loses its fascination with material things. A person on this level will not simply make it an issue of racist Europeans and their love for cotton and sugar.

A poet on this level will also have a healthy balance of material that will remind people of their gifts, how great they are, and how good it is to be alive. When you have great insight and hindsight, you will be able to better help your audience see your vision.

Chamber of Bodhi

The final chamber is the Chamber of Bodhi. Bodhi is a Sanskrit word for "awakening" or "enlightenment." This chamber is related to thought or consciousness. In this chamber, you have become one with the source, your art, and your audience. You are able to command stages, change minds, uplift spirits, educate, and inspire others to reach their full potential.

At this level, you have an awareness of the true nature of the universe. Once attained, you will have stopped the cycle of Samsara (reincarnation). Some believe that there is nothing new under the sun. I don't believe this. To believe that statement, one would have to believe that creation has exhausted all possibilities and everything has been talked about. If you believe in infinite possibilities, then your audience shouldn't have to suffer from reincarnated poetry. Some themes are universal within the human experience: love, hate, heartbreak and suffering. But there are some topics that have not been explored or are seldom addressed.

You will know that you have reached the final level by the appearance of a sublime glow around you. Then and only then will you find the master within self. Also, you will be able to catch bullets with your teeth.

But remember, although you will have become a master of your craft, you are to be considered a student-master. A wise person understands that with all he knows, he still knows nothing at all. With that said, you will until your dying day be in the process of learning. Who knows, after it's all said and done, you may even be able to recognize an eighth chamber. Time will tell.

Conclusion

If you stayed with me this long, then you are serious about poetry. I hope I have given a visual of what it means to be a poet in the 21st century and the philosophy that governs our art. To recap on the chambers and what they all mean, I will summarize below, stripping the chamber titles to their bare essence as follows:

• Chamber of study—study the workings of the universe and the history and styles of the art form.
• Chamber of experimentation—experiment with ways of expression using poetry to exercise those creative muscles in the brain.
• Chamber of life—life has no meaning if the person doesn't find purpose (either "destined" or self-proclaimed). Give your poems energy by having a clear direction and purpose. Here your poems will come more alive.
• Chamber of diversity—expand yourself into other genres of expression and come back with a new sense of direction. Become the poetry. Become your solutions. Go out and live a little to gain insight beyond what you've read.
• Chamber of performance—go out and perfect yourself at the open mics and features. Find your unique voice. Use your voice as a tool for change. Deliver your message in a way that resonates long after you're off stage.
• Chamber of intuition—poetry is an intuitive art form. You must be able to feel your way through concepts and not just logically construct your pieces. Use your third eye to see what others can't see and help them to see it as well.
• Chamber of The Last Dragon—the final glow. Become one with your poetry, audience and the universal creative spirit. Poetry is more than self-expression; it is a spiritual process that facilitates self-discovery. Only when you become one with the above six elements, will you be considered a master.

References:

Nina Simone
http://www.boscarol.com/nina/html/manual/bio.html
Shaolin Temple
http://shaolin-temple.gungfu.com/
Bruce Lee
http://en.wikipedia.org/wiki/Brucelee
Chakras
http://www.sacredcenters.com/

The Human Being: Universal Converter Of Ideas

"When imagination is in alignment with purpose"

What does it mean to be human? What was the purpose of our design? What specific tasks are we as human beings charged with to carry out for the good of the universe? What is our next evolutionary phase? These questions and more have been asked by sages and layman alike for centuries, and it seems as if the answers have been evading the human psyche for just as long. Humanity seems to have been dropped off on this earth with no instruction manual and no visible signs directing us on our journey to ensure our success. Sure, we can speculate as to what our job is individually, and some cultures have developed very sophisticated divination tools to ascertain a man's purpose, but can we answer these questions for humanity in general? Is there a theory that sounds plausible enough to get us closer to the answers we seek?

What are the physical limits of human beings? Are our limits predicated on how expansive our imaginations are? I think that these questions can be answered, and I think they already have to some degree. I am a firm believer that an object's purpose is determined by what it can do. The extent to how it can function is the purpose. I don't believe there is a "sole" purpose for anything. I believe everything serves multiple purposes. People limit themselves by constantly looking for the "one" thing as if human beings are one dimensional beings. Our body is made up millions of different parts and creatures (with their own consciousness) who together make up our physical body. Each individual task helps the whole body to complete various larger tasks. If we take our bodies as a que, then humanity itself is simply a collection of organisms or cells whose purpose is to work together to complete some larger tasks. But what are these tasks?

To be human is to be on a constant quest for meaning, and each new journey, each new obstacle in life, gets us closer to discovering that meaning for ourselves. I think the answers lie in the philosophy as espoused by our ancient African ancestors. They laid the foundations, which are encoded in their various cosmological myths, for us to build on and come closer to the answers we seek. My hypothesis is that human beings are simply vessels charged with the task of putting into form all that is possible outside of the natural world. I don't think there is any inherent meaning outside of that. I know it seems quite nihilistic, but I am not arguing that life doesn't have an inherent value nor am I trying to prove or disprove the existence of a higher being. What I am positing is that human beings were created simply to create and express that which lies dormant in the realm of ungrasped ideas, which other beings on this earth are not capable of doing due to the limits of their physical and mental capacities.

The World of Un-Grasped Ideas

Every African nation has its own dominant cosmological world view that shapes how they interact with each other in a community and the environment that surrounds them. While each ethnic group has its own unique characteristics, there is an underlying unity in ideas that allow us to safely label the following collective thoughts as essentially African. Some of these characteristics include reverence and the belief in ancestors as intermediaries between the Supreme Creative spirit and man; the essential importance of ritual to make accessible the power of spirit for uniting the community and to complete mundane tasks; their style of art; their method of kingship; their reverence for elders as critical assets for the structure of the whole community; and their proverbial method of teaching moral and ethical behavior and its usage during disputes.

One other thing a lot of African cultures have in common is how they see the structure of the "under world." The African world view essentially sees everything that exists in the universe as a form of energy (more recently realized in the field of quantum theory). This energy is usually separated into two planes or more: the ancestral realm and the physical realm. In other words, there is a plane of existence in which there are no creative activities going on and another where activities are carried out. Among those ethnic groups who subscribe to this train of thought are the Dogon, Dagara, Twa, Yoruba, Kmtjw (Egyptian), Akan, Akamba, Backwa and the Chagga.

Essentially, there is a realm in which only unformed matter and conscious-ness exist. In this realm, everything that could possibly be thought of exists just waiting to take form in the physical realm. From this plane is where we humans get all of our ideas. Dr. Malidoma Some (Dagara priest from Burkino Faso West Africa) in his work *Of Water and the Spirit*, pg. 203 states:

> Our minds know better than we are able and willing to admit the existence of many more things than we are willing to accept. The spirit and the mind are one. Their vision is greater, much greater than the vision we experience in the ordinary world. *Nothing can be imagined that is not already there in the outer and inner worlds.* Your mind is a responder; it receives. It does not make things up. It can't imagine what does not exist. The blessing in this is that you are your mind. That is also a curse. When you refuse to accept the real-ity of your mind, you refuse yourself, and that is bad. – Emphasis mine

In speaking on the Kongo's concept of the aspired "V," Dr. Kimbwandende Kia Bunseki Fu-Kiau in his seminal work *African Cosmology of the Bantu Kongo*, pg. 130, expresses this division between realms:

> Everything is a "V" because the beginning itself, or the big bang, explod-ed in the form of the "V." Because it is the bridging "wire" between think-ing-matter the human [muntu], and unthinking matter (the world and source of "ungrasped" ideas and images). The "Vee" is the basis of all inspirational realities such as great ideas, images, illustrations, inventions of all orders (including works of art), wars and conceptions, both biological and ideological as well.

A theory that has more recently gained acceptance in the field of quan-tum physics has been the foundation of African thought since before writ-ten records. This theory is that the universe is essentially made up of waves (called strings in quantum mechanics). These waves are the foundation of all the physical structures in the universe. Some of these waves are detectible (what you can see) and others are not easily detectable by the human senses. These waves carry with them information of all that is possible in the uni-verse. Human beings live in an ocean of waves/radiations. The human body acts like an antennae, which if tuned to the right frequencies, can essentially pick up and interpret these messages embedded in these waves. You have "voiced waved messages" and "voice-less waved messages." Voiced waved messages are messages that carry sounds within a human being's audible range. A voice-less waved message is this same message outside of audible range or a message that uses images (memories, dreams, etc).

Energy cannot be created or destroyed, so the messages don't disappear, they simply float around the universe waiting on a receiver to grasp it. Dr. Gabriel Oyibo, in his God Almighty Grand Unified Theorem, posits that the universe is essentially a force field of energy. Within this force field, energy is simply shifting back and forth between extremes. This supports the theory behind African divinations. Since information is always around, and simply moving somewhere in the universe, we should be able to access this information using the tools already present in the universe (hack into the Matrix). In regards to this topic of discussion, according to African philosophical thought, any and everything that could be imagined has already been invented and the secret to its formation lies dormant in the "spirit" realm waiting on a host to give it form.

The Meaning of Life: Expression

As Dr. Chiekh Anta Diop professed in an interview in the 1977 February issue of *Afriscope*, "Man's mission is creation (Van Sertima, 1986: 265)." Diop was expressing the typical African world view that man's essential nature is that of expression. My belief is that man was put here simply to express all of the ideas that lie dormant in the spirit realm or plane of existence. Man was created to be a converter of some sort to bring consciousness into fruition. It's sort of like how your computer works. There is an inherent language for your computer system in which all of the physical components understand each other and communicate with the motherboard. Well, the software used on any computer system doesn't understand raw computer language. This is why operating systems (Windows, Linux, Oracle, etc.) were invented to act as an intermediary between the software and the physical computer. So the software uses the operating system to harness the power of the computer to complete tasks or to bring ideas from the physical world into form on the computer screen. Human beings are essentially operating systems for the universe. We tap into the spiritual hard drive for ideas and make it visible by our worldly screens and share it on our physical internet.

So one of the most critical traits that must be developed in our people is our sense of creativity (the ability to take ideas and put them into form). As Diop has noted (Van Sertima, 1986: 265), the loss of our national sovereignty and slavery strangled our independent creativity. We essentially lost our ability to tap into the spirit world for ideas to work in our best interest. When we lost our sense of creativity, we essentially lost a part of ourselves; for in the indigenous world view, man is a vessel for creative expression.

Our ability to create is predicated on our willingness to expand the parameters of our imagination. As Albert Einstein has been quoted saying, "Imagination is more important than knowledge." Knowledge limits human potential, although it is the foundation on which all things that are to be come into fruition. Knowledge is the collection of facts based upon one's experience. The imagination is an initiatory experience of the mind that gives us a vision of what could be that doesn't already exist in physical form. Our ability to imagine must be accompanied by a strong belief that it could happen. Dr. Malidoma Some notes in his work *The Healing Wisdom of Africa*, pg. 66 that:

A harmonious relationship between Spirit and technology begins with trust in one's vision and one's perception. It proceeds through believing that what is commonly regarded as fantasy is not impossible, for instance that someone who dreams of becoming a bird can actually become one provided that he or she works at it and believes it as a reality. *Our vision is the starting point of a primal technological power, which is the ability to manifest, to make Spirit real in material form.* – Emphasis mine

He further brings this point home when he states:

The world of the Dagara doesn't distinguish between reality and imagination. To us, there is a close connection between thought and reality. To imagine something, to closely focus one's thoughts upon it, has the potential to bring that something into being. Thus, people who take a tragic view of life and are always expecting the worst usually manifest that reality. Those who expect that things will work together for the good usually experience just that. *In the realm of the sacred, this concept is taken even further, for what is magic but the ability to focus thought and energy to get results on the human plane?* The Dagara view of reality is large. *If one can imagine something, then it has at least the potential to exist.* — (Some 1998: 8) Emphasis mine

Imagination, Thought and Purpose

One of the other characteristics within the collective African thought is that human beings existed in some form, in another realm, and descended upon the earth from that realm. This descending upon the earth was attached with a purpose. For Malidoma:

> Individuals, as extensions of Spirit, come into the world with a purpose. At its core, the purpose of an individual is to bring beauty, harmony, and communion to Earth. Individuals live out their purpose through their work. Thus the human work of maintaining the world, to indigenous people, is an extension of the work that Spirit does to maintain the pulse of nature. The villager's quest for wholeness is an extension of nature's wholeness. (Some, 1998: 66)

My belief is that the main "purpose" of human beings is simply to bring into fruition the ideas already present in the Spirit realm. This idea, as can be seen, is nothing new to the realm of classical African thought. What I posit in addition to this theory is that when our thoughts and actions are in alignment with our purpose, this becomes the process in which our bodies become more and more sensitive to the subtle waves that encode what is possible in this realm. I believe that when the Spirit realm detects that a human being is in alignment with his/her purpose, and he or she has a healthy creative appetite, then the spirit world constantly sends this person ideas in hopes that it will give he/she form in the physical world (have you ever had so many great ideas but not enough time to carry them out?). This idea is supported by Some (1998: 78) in which he states:

> It is the indigenous understanding, however, that ideas you receive do not come from your imagination, they come from the Spirit World, and it is the spirits who will decide what the next step will be, what changes if any need to be made in technologies that they have given to you. A person's purpose is to serve, using that which has been put into his or her hands as a gift from Spirit.

As James Allen has noted (Allen, 1902: 37), "Until thought is linked with purpose there is no intelligent accomplishment." With African people, man's purpose is discovered using divination. Through the process of divination (if done before birth) a name is given, which is supposed to remind this person of their purpose and gifts to the community. If divination has not been done for a person, a simple studying of what a person gravitates to the most can guide one into understanding what their purpose is. Once that discovery has been made and internalized, then one should begin to think of ways on how to express and fulfill that purpose with new conventions and processes to improve the current state of humanity.

There are two dimensions to this discussion that must be addressed: 1) the theory that man's essential purpose is to bring into fruition the ideas that the creator has hidden in waves moving throughout the universe, and 2) that ideally man should want to bring into fruition the concepts that will bring the community and mankind fortune instead of misfortune. The indigenous don't necessarily believe in "good or bad." Instead, it is best to try to understand it in terms of fortune and misfortune. For something that is socially considered "good" (like a car) could also be considered "bad" (bad emissions that harm the environment and cause global warming). So as Malidoma has stated, we are here to bring into fruition concepts and structures that allow everything in the social and physical environments to work in harmony. According to the people of the Kongo, human beings [Bantu] are what they call, "systems of systems" (Fu-Kiau 2001; 70). We are entities that create systems, whether they be social or mechanical. This idea of being a system of a larger system speaks not only to the notion that there is a larger collective responsibility, but that we have the ability to create systems in the manner of the Supreme Creative Being.

There is a documentary film out now called *The Secret* that speaks about the universal Laws of Attraction. In the film you will find commentary by a Dr. Michael Beckworth who is the founder of the Agape International Spiritual Center in California. In a November 2, 2006 interview on CNN's Larry King Live show, Dr. Beckworth made an interesting and most profound comment. Larry King asked him, "Does God want us to be rich?" and this was his response:

> "We are here to deliver our gifts, our talents, and our capacities and develop ourselves to our fullest potential and express ourselves. Now the universe, the power, the presence, the love of God, whatever you want to call this presence, wants your structures stable, so that God can express more through you."

This again echoes the sentiment that if one is in alignment with one's purpose, then the spirit realm will send ideas your way for you to materialize in your lifetime. Not only does that quote reiterate that concept, but it also echoes the classical African world view that man is a vehicle for expression. So the church folk are right when they say, "let em use ya (you)," expressing the notion that human beings are the chosen vessels to express "God's" will.

So this idea isn't new and is understood on some level by most people in my opinion. Our job is to develop ourselves in a manner that allows our senses to make a bountiful catch of concepts when fishing in the cosmic ocean of ideas. Our bodies were designed to make manifest the potential that lies dormant in the universe. We must consciously choose to bring forth concepts that will work in harmony with nature (maat) and not bring isfet (disharmony, evil) to our communities. Our capacity to materialize great ideas is predicated on how expansive our imaginations are and is fueled by the power of belief.

For a good number of African Americans, things don't change in their lives because 1) they don't possess the creative faculties to dream up ways out of their current situations, and 2) they don't believe that the seemingly impossible is possible. This was the lesson as expressed through the Matrix Trilogy. Developing our creative faculties through art, music, dance, sculpting, inventions, poetry and a host of other creative endeavors trains our psyche to be able to tune our mind to the frequency of Spirit. Once we are in tune with Spirit, then we can make the music we were designed to orchestrate in which the Supreme Creative Spirit is the conductor.

References:

Allen, James (1902). *As a man thinketh*. Chicago, Lushena Books, Inc.

Diop, Cheikh Anta (1991). *Civilization or Barbarism: An Authentic Athropology*. New York, Lawrence Hill Books

Fu-Kiau, K. Kia Bunseki (2001). *African Cosmology of the Bantu Kongo: Principles of Life and Living*. Canada, Athelia Henrietta Press

Mbiti, John S (1989). *African Religions and Philosophy*. New Hampshire, Heinemann Educational Publishers

Sertima, Ivan Van (1986). *Great African Thinkers: Cheikh Anta Diop*. Tansaction Publishers, Morehouse College

Some, Malidoma (1998). *The Healing Wisdom of Africa*. New York, Penguin Putman, Inc.

Some, Malidoma (1994). *Of Water and the Spirit*. New York, Penguin Putman, Inc.

Satan Isn't Such A Bad Guy

I have been in recent discussions concerning personal interpretations of spiritual concepts and their applications in our everyday lives. I interact with various practitioners of many spiritual systems, and of course, many people have numerous interpretations on various concepts within those systems. So the question came up on how to correctly interpret what we call "negative" forces in our lives and how to properly apply the understanding of those forces so that one can grow and use that knowledge effectively within one's spiritual system.

In times of antiquity, the developers of spiritual systems created detailed myths to better explain concepts in nature. Over time, to keep the teachings in tact, they developed priesthoods in which the teachings could be properly explained for those willing to learn and who were ready for initiation into becoming an elder (priest). To explain abstract concepts in nature, the creators simplified these concepts and personified the energy forces so that it could be easily understood by the initiate.

For example, in the Ta-Merrian Shetaut Neter (Hidden mysteries of the Netchers – gods), what Egyptologist call "gods," are actually energy forces and concepts in nature. *Shu* represents Air. *Geb* represents the Earth. *Nut* represents the Sky. *Het Heru* represents the life energy in the universe, and *Tefnut* represents moisture. So when you read about these Netchers (gods) in the Egyptian myths, understand them better as forces in nature and how they interact with each other (like how sunlight is used in plants to undergo a process called photosynthesis, which transforms light into energy for the plants). If we keep this concept in mind, we can better understand what the ancient writers were trying to tell us in these stories they created.

A historical overview

The oldest recorded spiritual system is that of the Nile Valley Africans, which became widely practiced between the times of 10,000 and 4100 BCE. The stories of Ra, Asar, Aset, Set, Nebthet, Anpu and Heru became well known in ancient Egypt and went through many transformations. These systems were always concerned with the laws of opposites and the building of strong character (keep that in mind).

One of the major characters in the Asar, Aset and Heru drama of ancient Ta-Meri (Egypt) was that of Set. Remember that in spiritual myths, the gods represented forces in nature and were not actual personages; so the most important thing is what each character in the myth represented, more so than who they were and what spiritual system expressed that energy.

Set is the brother of Asar and the uncle of Heru. The myth of Asar, Aset and Heru is quite long and I will not go into the details here. A good book I recommend to get some understanding of the story is Dr. Muata Ashby's *Resurrecting Osirus*. Set, because of his egoistic nature, murders his brother Asar and attempts to usurp the thrown of Kmt (Egypt). Set represents the lower nature in mankind. He is intelligence without wisdom. He is impulsiveness and reckless passionate behavior that stunts the spiritual growth of every human being. Set was adopted by the Greeks and called Seth. Set later was brought into the Christian myth and renamed Satan. In the Christian system, Satan is the personification of evil and is the sole entity responsible for the entire world's suffering.

An ancient perspective

In ancient myths, the objective was not to look at the characters in the stories as distant personages who have these worthwhile experiences that don't relate to us. The objective was for the initiate to internalize the characters and relate them to one's life. Set and Heru are not different people; they are aspects of YOU reading the story. Set represents YOUR lower nature and the story is designed to show you how to have your lower nature serve your higher, more divine nature (Heru, Asar, Aset).

The same objective was expressed in the Christian myth through the story of Satan. Satan has been given many names and attributes. His most notable are devil and demon. I think it is time we define what these terms mean and trace their etymological roots to get a better understanding of their purposes.

Devil comes from the Greek word diabolos "slanderer," lit. "one who throws (something) across" the path of another.

Demon comes from the Greek daimonion, a "divine principle or inward oracle."

The definitions of these words, when contemplated deeply, have connotations that were not understood by those who were not initiated into the priesthood. Modern churches today have given a false perception of what Satan is and his function in our lives according to the ancients. I hope to bring about a paradigm shift in thinking so that we may use the "Satan" energy to our benefit.

The purpose of Satan

Today, people take myths literally and it has done a disservice to the spiritual community because proper interpretation hasn't been explained to the laymen. People think that an entity named Satan exists and he is the "enemy" of God. They believe there is an intergalactic war between God and his creation. But they never stop to think that if Satan was so bad, why hasn't God gotten rid of him yet? For those that believe in the Bible, why would God kill humanity off several times (Noah and the flood, Sodom and Gomorrah, etc.), but not get rid of the "person" responsible for the evil? The reason why is because Satan represents a fundamental concept in nature. For there to be good, there must be bad. There is no cold without hot, here without there, large without small. To destroy Satan would be to destroy creation itself, for what will you reference when you speak about all things "good?" There is no "good" without "evil."

We are here on earth to have experiences that are designed for the development of higher consciousness. There is no growth without struggle. What we call evil is put in this realm to force us to strive for things better; otherwise we get complacent and there is no spiritual growth. This is the "secret" behind the Garden of Eden story. It was a myth to explain to the initiates that in perfection, there is death (no growth). Satan was used as a force to kick man out of his comfort zone so he could have experiences that promote spiritual growth and understanding.

If you notice, in the Bible Satan doesn't commit any acts; man does all of the evil. People misinterpret influence and choice with actions that are forced. All Satan ever did was give mankind a choice to do right or wrong. This leads us back to our first definition of devil (one who throws something across the path of another). The usage of the word devil is a pun on its definition. When someone throws (speaks) something at you, they are bringing your attention to an idea. We say it all the time in common speech: "Hey son, let me throw something at you real quick!" All you are saying is "Let me introduce you to this concept or option."

So the "devil's" job is to give us options, to give us situations in which we are forced to use our free will and make a choice. His other characteristic is that of a demon. The word demon comes from "daimonion," which means divine principle or inward oracle. This lets us know that it is not an external entity, but an internal being that is trying to tell us something.

If God is divine and all things it creates is divine, and if he created Satan, then Satan is divine and serves a divine purpose. Satan forces you to realize the inconsistencies in your own character so that you can address those issues. He brings these issues to surface. This is divine because he gets you to admit that it was YOU that did that bank robbery, not some invisible spirit. It was YOU that was cheating on your husband, not some demon. It was YOU that bought that liquor bottle; it wasn't 50 Cent that made you do it.

It is like pain in your body. Pain is a mechanism in your body that tells the brain that there is an area of the body that is not in harmony with the whole. The brain is supposed to recognize where the problem is and signal to the spirit that we need to address this quickly or something very damaging is going to happen to our body. You wouldn't call the pain in your stomach "evil;" it is simply doing its job, and although painful for you, it is a necessary component of existing. It is a very smart mechanism of the body. If we didn't have pain, people would just drop dead with no warning because something was wrong and there was nothing to signal to self that something was wrong in the first place.

Conclusion

When you can admit that you are the reason for all of your wrongdoing, then you are ready for initiation. You have now matured to the point in which spiritual development can take place. Satan is not bad. He is actually necessary in this realm of existence. It just takes a paradigm shift in your thinking to understand what a Set, Seth, Satan is supposed to represent in nature and to use that knowledge to your advantage and grow with the experience.

In the story of Aset, Asar and Heru, Set isn't destroyed; he is made to steer the boat of Ra and protect the boat from Chaos. In the story, Set is used for good purposes. It is made the servant of righteousness. Set/Satan cannot be destroyed, but he/it can be tamed.

Next time you eat that foot-long hoagie, remember why your heart started hurting. It was from the development of acid reflux, which is really Set, (Satan, Seth) letting you know that you made a not-so-beneficial decision and you need to correct this soon. Set's, (Satan's) job is to provide us with choices to exercise our free will so we can overcome obstacles to develop spiritually, and Set forces us to admit our shortcomings so we can be ready for spiritual transformation. And for this, we must understand that that energy force is neither bad nor good, it is what it is.

* This discussion draws from many traditions from my early studies with the ICUPK (Hebrew Isrealites), lectures from Jabade Powell, and the Greek document called "The Virgin of the World" which is their account of the Asarian Resurrection drama.

Feelings Are Good Servants
But Poor Masters

The title of this article speaks to the issue of emotions and when the embracement of emotions are beneficial at certain times more so than others. The implication of the Kemetic proverb above (the title) is that while emotions serve as good agents of self-realization and as a catalysts for change, they are poor instruments for making critical decisions in our lives. This topic is important for people to understand for many decisions are made concerning the lives of millions of people and many of them are based purely on emotions and not objective reason. It seems like too many people simply make decisions based on feelings they have (which are based on their cultural beliefs) instead of those decisions being made because they are of benefit and they restore balance into society. Or, they come to conclusions on a given topic without examining exactly what is being said because they let their emotions cloud their ability to see what the core issues are. We will attempt to address these issues and more in this article.

Definitions

Before any discussion can begin, it is always wise to define key concepts that serve as the framework of that discussion. The New Lexicon Webster's Dictionary defines emotion as "a strong feeling (such as fear, wonder, love, sorrow, shame) often accompanied by a physical reaction (e.g. blushing or trembling)"; Emotional as "of or relating to the emotions || showing deep feeling or emotion (an emotional farewell) || aimed at the arousing of emotion (e.g. his patriotic argument is purely emotional) ruled by emotion rather than by reason.

To make things clearer, emotions are the outward vibratory expressions of the human condition. These feelings or emotions are humanity's internal way of making consciousness aware of the severity of a given situation. So being emotional is as natural as breathing. But the problem with emotions (like the senses) is that it is set up to guide decisions, not make them. This is why it is a good servant but poor master.

Underlying Issues

When in an intellectual conflict or trying to get to the root of a problem, emotions cloud one's ability to see the true issue at hand and hinder one's intellectual capacity to resolve the problem. Biologically, this is the result of cortisol being released into the system at times of stress. It is nature's safeguard against rationalism when it is not needed. For example, if a truck was headed your way at full speed, it would be a bad time to try and calculate the velocity of the truck's speed and approximately how long it has to reach you.

This is the result of egoism (as defined by German philosopher Fitche) and humanity's inability to think beyond one's own human experiences. People assume that their experiences and thinking processes is the norm or standard for how humanity as a whole should operate and think. So when information comes that appear to be in opposition to their experiences, they immediately try to combat the supposed opposition from their emotional reserve instead of with their cognitive faculties. When people debate issues, usually one or more parties in the debate, because of their inability to not be emotional, throws the whole discussion off with information that is not relevant to the debate. This in turn distorts the real issue at hand because both parties are now engaged in a debate that has no correlation to the topic and has no way of reaching the real issues and how to resolve those issues.

Some Examples

Ebony Phonics debate, December 18, 1996: Many African-Americans were upset at the Oakland Unified School District's recognition of African American Vernacular English (Ebonics) as a unique language stature in the context of their district's African-American population. African-American adults were outraged at the resolution because they thought the school district was going to teach their children Ebony Phonics over English. They also felt that it was a personal attack on them as African-Americans to say that their children can't speak English. Now Ebony Phonics is used as a joke in high class circles, as people unknowingly showing how ignorant they are on the issue.

Ebonics has been studied for more than 40 years and is not a new phenomenon. What linguists have overwhelmingly concluded is that the African American language systems have origins in West and Niger-Congo languages and are not merely dialects of English. The general population may think that they are saying it's a different language all together, but to linguists and educators it is viewed in this context: that language varieties may fuse different language donor sources in a formation of a distinctive variety of languages. This is the case with Ebonics and this is normal and is pretty universal. One hypothesis of the origin of African American English posits a link with creoles found in the African Diaspora (e.g. Sierra Leone Krio, Jamaican Creole, Gullah). So when African Americans were lashing out against the resolution to recognize the distinct language stature, they were lashing out against knowledge of self and information of their own cultural heritage. They were lashing out utilizing their inner hatred for anything African being taught in the public school system.

That was the underlying issue. It was about teaching something about African history and culture and using that as a tool and a basis to teach African American children how to master the English language. It was set up for children to recognize and appreciate their unique heritage and language structure, but African American adults couldn't see the underlying issue because they were thinking with their emotions (their embarrassment of being Africans) rather than with their heads. This issue is worthy of an article itself, which I will write later, and to read the original resolution (which most African Americans didn't) you can visit

http://www.linguistlist.org/topics/ebonics/ebonics-res2.html

Separation of Church and State: This is a hot topic amongst many circles and especially amongst Christian church goers. I for one am for separation of church and state because being an historian, I have a more in-depth view as to the wider implications at hand and how the merge can cause more harm than good. I am not here to argue the merits, just to point out how emotionalism prevents resolution for people who oppose each other.

Lately Christians feel that Christianity is being attacked by "pagan" religious systems because everywhere they go, their symbols are being taken down, by force of legislation, off of public property. Now Christians are outraged that someone would even be offended at their symbolism and have voiced their opinions quite loudly at each and every incident in which a symbol was ordered down. Usually the people who are in opposition do not have a clear grasp of the purpose of having your governmental entity separate from your religious system, nor do they comprehend the dangers of those merging (especially in a society with more than 50 named religions).

They never take the time to try and understand the opposing person's view or try to understand what the real issue is. One of the major issues is which religion gets precedence over other religious systems when it comes time for symbolic representation on public buildings? Are you willing to have every religion represented in the halls of Congress, including people who are Satanists? What does your religious symbol mean to people who are not in your religion? The latter question is the one that stands out the most to me. For a Christian may see a picture of the Bible and the cross as symbols of peace and love; however, I see it as a symbol of deceit, destruction and murder. You may not agree with how I view Christian symbols, but my views are shared by many whose forefathers were the victims of governments who used their interpretation of Christianity to make their lives hell. Slavery should be the first example that comes to mind. The Jewish Holocaust is another one that comes to mind. The Crusades, Jim Crow, the murder of Canaanites and the murder of the African Ethiopian Jews by the Church of Rome in the first through third centuries are just a few examples of destruction conceived, funded and executed by Christianity's leaders and followers. But Christians who oppose the separation of church and state don't oppose it because they know this history, they oppose because it is their religion and it is up to them to defend the sanctity of that religion by any means necessary without logically thinking about the power of symbolism and how it can and has been used to oppress people of different cultures and ideologies.

Public buildings and agencies are funded by public dollars. Your public dollars are supposed to be a representation of the ideals of the collective body of citizens and how they tackle social problems that affect the corporate community. Your tax dollar is supposed to be a mediator between a corporate need and its resolution (fire department, public schools, city hall, court systems, etc.). These public agencies, in a spirit of fairness and harmony of society, cannot show favor in any manner of one class of citizens over the other. This is the issue and not how you feel anyone is attacking you. People want equal representation, and people don't find it fair that their contribution is not recognized just like other people who contribute or contribute more.

Humanity has proven, to me, that it hasn't matured as of yet (even though we have been in existence for more than 4.2 million years) and until we have, we can't have the people in power making decisions based on their cultural and religious values without it being beneficial to others outside their circle. This is why you have separation of church and state, because people just can't act right and it is a remedy to a past social ill. Now we all don't have to agree, but we have to come to a conclusion that leaves the society in a balanced state. The only way you can get to that conclusion is to not be emotional and think rationally.

So what iz we gone do?

Well the answer to that is quite simple: Think objectively (yeah I know impossible), gather all relevant information, avoid ad hominem attacks, keep the principles of MAAT (peace, balance, harmony, righteousness) and understanding as the desired result. If these objectives are adhered to, any debate or conflict can be resolved in a fair manner. While being emotional is a natural human trait and is in no way shunned by the author, as one matures, the benefits of logical, rational thought almost always outweighs being emotional when it comes to conflict resolution and bringing life back into balance for the benefit of all mankind.

A Dialogue Of Energy

The crux of most, if not all, African spiritual systems lie in the understanding of the laws that govern how energy works. These energy forces are usually personified in myths, and these myths instruct us in unique ways about how these forces interact. What we call Mdw Ntr (Medu Netcher) or the Orishas are in reality varying degrees of energy principles that are the very fabric of a continuing creation. It is believed that these energy forces are used to make manifest concepts already in existence since before the first "occasion." It is within man's power to call out to these energy forces to complete tasks here on earth.

These principles and more have been conceptualized and practiced since before recorded history, and to this date, remain integral to the spiritual development of man. In traditional African spiritual systems, there are formal ways in which one can harness these energy forces for one's personal benefit: to shift one's state from misfortune to fortune (Ire). Aspects of these energy forces are called ancestors and they can work on your behalf and inform you of situations that may be of benefit to you. It is believed that what we call ancestors are deceased former members of society who are in another realm now connected to the "source." Since we don't have a reference for the source (because the source in its totality is beyond human conception), all we can do is refer to that aspect of the source (because all that exists is the source) we call ancestors.

When members of society die, they now exist in a realm where there is no differentiation (but a singularity) and all knowledge is known. That's why you can call on ancestors because they now have 360 degrees of knowledge (simply meaning complete). Those familiar with ancient Ta-Merrian mythos have heard of Asar and are familiar with the double ostrich feathers worn with the White Crown of Upper Kmt by Asar after his death. Ostrich feathers were chosen in this instance because an ostrich can turn its head 360 degrees. This was perfect to convey the concept of seeing (knowing) all that exists and one cannot know all that exists until one has experienced death. The latter lesson is also taught in the value of the left of eye of Heru which symbolically is broken down into various parts (63/64), which was torn out by Set in their many battles. It represents an incompleteness that cannot be filled until one dies.

Moreover, the methodologies used to access these spiritual forces are universal throughout Africa. We will look at how the practitioners of Ifa, while preparing sacred space, call upon these ancestral energy forces during prayer invocations and how that same methodology is used to harness the power of information manipulation in modern software programs (using Microsoft's .Net as an example). We will take an example from Awo Fa'Lokun Fatunmbi, owner   of   the   Awo   Study   Center   website, (http://www.awostudycenter.com/Articles/artancestors1.htm).

Usually, this ritual is done at an ancestor shrine made in the home of the practitioner. According to Fatunmbi, "Most Ifa prayers start by addressing a particular Spirit, followed by an identification of the person who is making the prayer as follows:

> Iba se Egun
>
> *I pay homage to the spirit of the ancestors.*
> Emi (your name) Omo (list your lineage starting with your parents and
>   working backwards)
> *I am* (your name) *child of* (lineage)

This opening portion of the prayer is followed by a blessing of the leaves as follows.

> Iba se Ori ewe, (I pay homage to the Spirit of the Leaves.)
> *After the leaves have been blessed, ask them to perform a specific task.*
> Ire alafia, (The good fortune of peace,)
> Ire'lera, (the good fortune of a stable home,)
> Ire ori're. (the good fortune of wisdom.)

The prayer concludes with a statement of thanks.

> Ewe, mo dupe, ase. (Leaves, I thank you, so be it.)"

Basically it can be broken down like this:

- **Open** prayer by stating what energy you are calling (in this case ancestors)
- **Identify** who you are and who you belong to (family lineage)
- **Instruct** what tasks are to be completed
- **Close** the prayer and formally end in "ase (ashe)"

Awo Fatunmbi goes on to say:

> "[Ending in "to" (pronounced "tow")]… This is known as placing your
> ase on the prayer. The word functions as a seal locking the prayer on to
> the object that is being blessed. The word also indicates an end to the
> invocation, so that words spoken after the end of the prayer are not
> heard by Spirit as part of the prayer."

Software programs operate very similarly to the Ifa invocation mentioned above. We will look at an example using Microsoft's web programming language ASP.NET. In this example, we are just going to call on a script that retrieves information from a database generated by Adobe's Dreamweaver.

```
<%@ Page Language="VB" ContentType="text/html"
ResponseEncoding="iso-8859-1" %>

<MM:DataSet
id="DataSet1"
runat="Server"
IsStoredProcedure="false"
ConnectionString='<%#System.Configuration.ConfigurationSettings.
    AppSettings("MMCONNECTIONSTRINGconnTrendsetters")
    %>'

DatabaseType='<%#
System.Configuration.ConfigurationSettings.AppSettings("MMCONN
    ECTIONDATABASETYPEconnTrendsetters") %>'
CommandText='<%# "SELECT arauthor, ardate, artitle, ID FROM
    6degrees" %>'
PageSize="10"
Debug="true">
```

```
<EditOps>
<EditOpsTable Name="6degrees" />
<Parameter Name="ID" Type="Integer" IsPrimary="true"
/></EditOps>
</MM:DataSet>
```

We will break it down like this:

- The [**<%@**] portion is the **Opening** section of the code.
- The [Page Language="VB" ContentType="text/html" ResponseEncoding="iso-8859-1" %>] **Identifies** what code this is and what family of code it descends from; in this case we are VB (Visual Basic) script.
- The code in the middle basically says, "Hey, connect to this database [connTrendsetters]{the ancestral realm} of information and I want you to specifically go to the table "6degrees" [ancestor] and pull out this information so we can use it for some other stuff explained in some more code below." This would be the **Instructions**.
- </MM:DataSet> formally **Closes** this section of the code.

Anything written after </MM:DataSet> is ignored by the compiler looking at this section of the code responsible for accessing our database, just like any words said after "to" or "ase" in the prayer mentioned above are ignored by the spirit. These are essentially two methods for accessing and manipulating information/energy for our personal benefit. The same concepts used to gain information from the ancestral realm is (with slight modifications) the exact method used in computer programming. Although the languages may be different, it still follows the same basic pattern. All programming languages follow this procedure.

This shows us the underlying unity of laws that govern the dialogue of energy forces and how they interact with each other. This is expressed in the Hermetic principle of correspondence, which states, "As above, so below. So below, as above." In Quantum Chaos Theory, this same principle is called "scalar self-similarity." Self-similarity implies recursion or a pattern within a pattern. In biology and philosophy this is called a "holon." Arthur Koestler describes it as "something that has integrity and identity at the same time as it is a part of a larger system, it is a subsystem of the larger system." What we see in a world of what appears to be differentiation, is an underlying unity that governs the "ebb and flow" of life. The laws that govern one system apparently govern a seemingly different system.

So just know that the next time you visit a website or pull up Microsoft Word to do a task, you are essentially calling on your ancestors by a method discovered by African people at a time when there were no written records. I now close this essay with </Ashe>

The Meaning Of Life

I DON'T KNOW!

When I Think Of Poetry

I think of v-8 engine pens with the power of 6 cylinders
That process thoughts at the speed of 3 digit integers
With a torque equal to hurricane and earthquake forces
That can pull a community together with about 350 horses
Of diesel fuel-injected Africana type perspectives
That inspires students to take quantum physics as an elective

When I think of poetry
I think of a series of metaphors, folklores and fables
Whose elements when arranged resemble the periodic table
Of its own elements in sequence like sulfur, chlorine and argon
Instead, our charts are filled with subjects, predicates and prepositions
As potassium has an ionization potential at 4.341
Poetry has a microphone melting potential
   at 360 degrees of spiritual perfection

When I think of poetry
I think of wordsmiths meditating in Shaolin temples in China
Training, carrying water buckets up steep hills, barefoot
   like a mountain climber
Spitting Wu-Tang sword-style verbs on one foot with their arms folded
While practicing the crane style, while Master Chin yells
   in their ear and their pride's scolded
All in preposition to get the young Monks ready to fight
Jetting with lightening speed on horseback just to spit at an open mic

When I think of poetry…..

My People Are Destroyed For A Lack Of Science (Imhotep 4:6)

I often get into heated discussions on such topics as religion, politics, social matters and history. What I run into often (and I have been guilty at times as well) is engaging in discussions with individuals who have not researched the topic thoroughly enough to have a healthy discussion. We often take for granted certain information we deem as facts. Sometimes we never question a concept at its base level to get a better understanding of what is trying to be conveyed by the event or statement. A lot of times we believe in something simply because everybody else believes it. We have the notion that everyone else supports this, so it must be true. We get caught up in the hype of someone famous endorsing an idea or that person being an authority on the subject, as if their analysis cannot be flawed. We often ignore flaws that have been pointed out by someone of less notoriety than the famous individual.

This is the crime committed by most when it comes to their religious choices, health or philosophical world views. Our current condition in this country is directly related to our lack (as a whole) of systematically researching and gathering information on how to combat social ills with the intent of passing on the knowledge to successive generations. We'd rather leave it up to the "experts" and believe "their" opinions without seeing if their analysis stands up to scrutiny.

I am not in any manner negating the hundreds of individuals who are engaged in this type of fact finding process. What I am saying is that it is not to the level that it is a part of the cultural psyche to engage in this type of research activity. It is not customary for us as a people to breakdown any and all information to its base level to get the full understanding. We shun individuals who have a tendency to be scientific in their information gathering. Have you ever been in a conversation and someone has asked you, "Why do you always have to analyze everything?" I say, "Why not?" When it comes to education, history, archeology, philosophy, psychiatry, religion, and politics, we cannot afford to be anything less then scientific in our analysis. When we understand that the decisions we make on a day to day basis impacts the lives of hundreds of people whom we may never meet, we should want to ensure that the decisions we make are based on solid knowledge and not based solely on our emotions (does Iraq come to mind for anyone?).

Example from the Bible

I will tell you off the top that I am not a Christian (as in the modern sense) and I don't profess to be an authority on Biblical affairs. This example is only used because most are familiar with Christian tenants. If any of you have ever read the Bible and have went to the book of Hosea, chapter four verse six states: "My people are destroyed for lack of knowledge: because thou hast rejected knowledge, I will also reject thee, that thou shalt be no priest to me: seeing thou hast forgotten the law of thy God, I will also forget thy children."

I have done the unthinkable (as if it has not already been done) and have replaced the word "knowledge" with the word "science." Before you start quoting scripture and start to throw stones at me, understand what is happening. The root word of knowledge is "know." To know means, "to perceive directly; grasp in the mind with clarity or certainty" [2]. Science comes from the Latin word "scientia," which means "to know" [3]. These words mean the exact same thing, so we can use them interchangeably. I like the word science better because it implies something much deeper then simply "to know." Science implies a systematic methodology for obtaining information. It is a process that is rigorous and helps us to understand phenomena better through trial, error, record keeping and analysis.

The Israelites were always in trouble with God (according to the Bible) and the environment because they didn't understand the concept of science and how it would help them in the long run. They didn't bother to research the scriptures and their deeper meanings in relation to the world around them. They were too busy being "spiritual" and refused the knowledge of the "world," for the "laws of God" are the "laws of nature."

Our people are in that same state of mind today. The scriptures say in 1 Corinthians 1:22, "For the Jews require a sign, and the Greeks seek after wisdom." The masses of our people, for the most part, do not want to engage in the type of activity needed to get us out of our educational, historical, philosophical, spiritual, psychological and health predicament. A lot of people allow their religion to dictate what knowledge is and what it isn't. Because of this, they never get to experience the wisdom and body of knowledge the world has to offer unless it comes from their "spiritual" sources. These are the same individuals who will never unlock nature's secrets because they despise science and view "carnal" knowledge as the work of the devil. Simply put, they hate logic.

What science entails

There is good science, there is pathological science, and then there is pseudoscience (which is, simply, a theory, methodology, or practice that is considered to be without scientific foundation) [1].

Pseudoscience is the science most so-called philosophers, historians and religious leaders are engaged in. They come up with theories and concepts and feed them to the people as truth without any substantial evidence whatsoever. For example, so-called religious scholars claim you can prove some of the Bible's stories, such as the flood, as actual historic events. They claim the event of Noah's flood is true because satellite pictures taken from space looking down on Mt. Ararat show a figure that appears to be a boat. Keep in mind they haven't actually gone up the mountain to find the boat and their whole claim is based on an image from outerspace. Whether the event happened is still up for debate. But you can't write articles, books or conduct sermons and tell people that the event is true based on evidence that doesn't exist. That's just plain lying. You have found no artifacts. No one concluded that it was a boat on the mountain. It is just pure heresy.

Another example is this concept of race. There is no scientific proof that race exists. There is nothing on the molecular level that you could definitively use to distinguish differentiation amongst human beings (so-called Black, Yellow, Red and White races). Race is a social construct of "racist" Europeans to aid in the suppression of African advancement and history in the world. To claim there is such a thing as race is unscientific and those who attempt to uphold the notion are engaged in pseudo science.

The term "pathological science" was coined by Nobel-laureate chemist Irving Langmuir in a lecture he gave at General Electric's Knolls Atomic Power Laboratory in 1953. With pathological science, there is no dishonesty involved, but people are tricked into false results by a lack of understanding about what human beings can do to themselves in the way of being led astray by subjective effects, wishful thinking or threshold interactions [4].

Many people do not know how to discern truth from falsehood. This is what is missing in most discourses in which the outcome can be obscured (religion, history, cultural anthropology, etc.). The following serves as a guide to aid the reader in being able to do just that in a scientific manner.

Peter Sturrock, Professor of Space Science at Stanford University in California, offered the following as guidelines to those dealing with anomalous phenomena:

(1) In studying any phenomenon, face up to the strongest evidence you can find, even if it is in conflict with current orthodoxies.

(2) Go to the original sources for your data. Do not trust secondary sources.

(3) Deal with "degrees of belief," which can be conveniently characterized by probabilities. It is important to avoid assigning probability P=0 (complete disbelief) or P=1 (complete certainty) to any proposition since if you adopt either of these values, that value can never be changed no matter how much evidence you subsequently receive.

(4) Focus on evidence and testing.

(5) Subdivide the work into categories so different people take on different tasks.

(6) Where possible work in teams; first because a combination of expertise may be required, and secondly, because a team is more likely to be self-correcting than someone working alone.

(7) In theoretical analyses, list all assumptions. This seems a simple, innocuous request, yet it will not always be easy to put into effect. [5]

Although the above (and to follow) deal mainly with physics, its principles can be applied to any other area of study also. Michael Shermer listed 25 fallacies that lead us to believe weird things:

(1) Theory influences observation. Heisenberg wrote, "What we observe is not nature itself but nature exposed to our method of questioning." Our perception of reality is influenced by the theories framing our examination of it.

(2) The observer changes the observed. The act of studying an event can change it, an effect particularly profound in the social sciences, which is why psychologists use blind and double-blind controls.

(3) Equipment constructs results. How we make and understand measure-

ments is highly influenced by the equipment we use.

(4) Anecdotes do not make science. Stories recounted in support of a claim are not scientific without corroborative evidence from other sources or physical proof of some sort.

(5) Scientific language does not make a science. Dressing up a belief in jargon, often with no precise or operational definitions, means nothing without evidence, experimental testing, and corroboration.

(6) Bold statements do not make claims true. The more extraordinary the claim, the more extraordinarily well-tested the evidence must be.

(7) Heresy does not equal correctness. Being laughed at by the mainstream does not mean one is right. The scientific community cannot be expected to test every fantastic claim that comes along, especially when so many are logically inconsistent. If you want to do science, you have to learn to play the game of science. This involves exchanging data and ideas with colleagues informally, and formally presenting results in conference papers, peer-reviewed journals, books, and the like.

(8) Burden of proof. It is the person who makes the extraordinary claim who has the burden of proving the validity of the evidence.

(9) Rumors do not equal reality. Repeated tales are not of necessity true.

(10) Unexplained is not inexplicable. Many people think that if they themselves cannot explain something that it must be inexplicable and therefore a true mystery of the paranormal.

(11) Failures are rationalized. In science, the value of negative findings is high, and honest scientists will readily admit their mistakes. Pseudoscientists ignore or rationalize failures.

(12) After-the-fact reasoning. Also known as "post hoc, ergo propter hoc," literally "after this, therefore because of this." At its basest level, this is a form of superstition. As Hume taught us, the fact that two events follow each other in sequence does not mean they are connected causally. Correlation does not mean causation.

(13) Coincidence. In the paranormal world, coincidences are often seen as deeply significant. As the behavioral psychologist B.F. Skinner proved in the laboratory, the human mind seeks relationships between events and often finds them even when they are not present.

(14) Representativeness. As Aristotle said, "The sum of the coincidences equals certainty." We forget most of the insignificant coincidences and remember the meaningful ones. We must always remember the larger context in which a seemingly unusual event occurs, and we must always analyze

unusual events for their representiveness of their class of phenomena.

(15) Emotive words and false analogies. Emotive words are used to provoke emotion and sometimes to obscure rationality. Likewise, metaphors and analogies can cloud thinking with emotion and steer us onto a side path. Like anecdotes, analogies and metaphors do not constitute proof. They are merely tools of rhetoric.

(16) Ad ignoratum. This is an appeal to ignorance or lack of knowledge, where someone claims that if you cannot disprove a claim it must be true. In science, belief should come from positive evidence, not a lack of evidence for or against a claim.

(17) Ad hominem and tu quoque. Literally "to the man" and "you also," these fallacies redirect the focus from thinking about the idea to thinking about the person holding the idea. The goal of an ad hominem attack is to discredit the claimant in hopes that it will discredit the claim. Similarly for tu quoque. As a defense, the critic is accused of making the same mistakes attributed to the criticized, and nothing is proved one way or the other.

(18) Hasty generalization. In logic, the hasty generalization is a form of improper induction. In life it is called prejudice. In either case, conclusions are drawn before the facts warrant it.

(19) Overreliance on authorities. We tend to rely heavily on authorities in our culture, especially if the authority is considered to be highly intelligent. Authorities, by virtue of their expertise in a field, may have a better chance of being right in that field, but correctness is certainly not guaranteed, and their expertise does not necessarily qualify them to draw conclusions in other areas.

(20) Either-or. Also known as the fallacy of negation or the false dilemma, this is the tendency to dichotomize the world so that if you discredit one position, the observed is forced to accept the other. A new theory needs evidence in favor of it, not just against the opposition.

(21) Circular reasoning. Also known as fallacy of redundancy, begging the question, or tautology, this occurs when the conclusion or claim is merely a restatement of one of the premises.

(22) Reductio ad absurdum and the slippery slope. Reductio ad absurdum is the refutation of an argument by carrying the argument to its logical end and so reducing it to an absurd conclusion. Surely, if an argument's consequences are absurd, it must be false. This is not necessarily so, though sometimes pushing an argument to its limits is a useful exercise in critical thinking; often this is a way to discover whether a claim has validity, especially

when an experiment testing the actual reduction can be run. Similarly, the slippery slope fallacy involves constructing a scenario in which one thing leads ultimately to an end so extreme that the first step should never be taken.

(23) Effort inadequacies and the need for certainty, control, and simplicity. Most of us, most of the time, want certainty, want to control our environment, and want nice, neat, simple explanations. Scientific and critical thinking does not come naturally, it takes training, experience, and effort. We must always work to suppress our need to be absolutely certain and in total control and our tendency to seek the simple and effortless solution to a problem.

(24) Problem-solving inadequacies. All critical and scientific thinking is, in a fashion, problem solving. There are numerous psychological disruptions that cause inadequacies in problem solving. We must all make the effort to overcome them.

(25) Ideological immunity, or the Planck Problem. In day-to-day life, as in science, we all resist fundamental paradigm change. Social scientist Jay Stuart Snelson calls this resistance an ideological immune system: "educated, intelligent, and successful adults rarely change their most fundamental presuppositions." As individuals accumulate more knowledge, theories become more well-founded, and confidence in ideologies is strengthened. The consequence of this, however, is that we build up an "immunity" against new ideas that do not corroborate previous ones. Historians of science call this the Planck Problem, after physicist Max Planck, who made this observation on what must happen for innovation to occur in science: "An important scientific innovation rarely makes its way by gradually winning over and converting its opponents: it rarely happens that Saul becomes Paul. What does happen is that its opponents gradually die out and that the growing generation is familiarized with the idea from the beginning. [6]"

(Liberally edited and paraphrased. M. Shermer, *Why People Believe Weird Things: Pseudoscience, Superstition, and Other Confusions of Our Time,* W.H. Freeman and Company, 1997)

Use this as a guide when conducting research. And more importantly, experiment. If you feel that a particular ideology is going to work (such as an economic plan) put it to the test. Go out and make it happen and then report your findings to the people. Don't engage in pseudo science. If it interests you, try to learn all you can about it. Learn to separate the "wheat" from the "shaft."

References:

[1], [4], [5]. [6], http://www.catchpenny.org/patho.html
[2] http://dictionary.reference.com/search?q=know
[3] http://dictionary.reference.com/search?q=science
Akbar, Nai'm. (1998) *Know Thyself.* Mind Production & Assoc;
Diop, Chiekh Anta. (1991). *Civilization or Barbarism: An Authentic
Anthropology.* Lawrence Hill Books

I Wanna, Love, Love, Love
Like This

A love like Malcolm and Betty type love. A love that says, baby I'll hold down the home front, while you go liberate the minds of our people cuz they need you type love. I need a love like, James and Florida Evans type, no matter how hard the period, or what conditions we live in, we can still find Good Times together type love. I need a Ramesis II type love. You know one of those, ain't no wife more beautiful than my Queen Nefertari, so I resurrect temples hewn out of granite stone mountains in Abu Simbel with statues to match type love.

I wanna, love love….love like that

That grandmamma and grandpapa type love. That we done watched four children and six great grand-children grow to become upright, productive gifts to humanity type love. That wait in a shoe store for three hours type love. That help you take out those thin micro braids type love. That when it's that time of the month I have the water bottle and heating pad ready before you go to sleep type love.

I wanna love that allows me to lie behind you in the bed, with my left arm around you because you like to sleep on your right side, and when you're half asleep and I reach over to give you a kiss, you slightly lift your butt up in the air, in that comfort zone only couples enjoy and ask me, "mmm whachu doing?" I wanna love that when we get into an argument, that I can call up your sister and try to find out what did I do wrong and what could I do to make it right type love. That me and her plot together a nefarious scheme to get us back together cuz you can get mad at me but can't stay mad at your sister type love.

See, I just wanna become your love, love….love like this

I can honestly say that I have never found a woman that could make me wanna love, love…love like this before. I mean I get all giddy when I receive a text message. I stay on the computer all night hoping that you log on so that maybe I could receive an instant message. I wanna buy you a New York style studio loft so you can have enough room and inspiration to paint when you're feeling creative. See, there's nothing wrong with having someone to hold, and when my eyes behold you in that t-shirt and those Leo panties, anything I had planned for that day is put on…hold. So, let's hold hands together at the dinner table as we say grace, because I have a lot to be thankful for, and I'm just blessed to share the same space with you

Breathe the same air as you
To occupy the same time zone
And praise the same God as you

Cuz I see the God in you and your name literally represents Christ consciousness. I wanna be your love, and when you're getting ready to spit at an open mic, I wanna be your extra boost of confidence. See love is sacrifice and there's nothing I wouldn't sacrifice for you…including my life. I sacrifice for you standing between two thieves like Jesus the Christ. I'll sacrifice my freedom like Harriet Tubman and keep going back through harm's way just so you can advance. I'll sacrifice telling you how I truly feel because I understand you still need time to heal and me wanting you all to myself would just be selfish. But I can't help it…I want us to be that personification of Method Man and Mary J Blige, you're all that I need type love. I want us to be that Luther Vandross and Cheryl Lynn if this world were mine type love. I want us to be that Winnie waiting 27 years for Nelson Mandela type love. In other words, I wanna be your love, cuz you are love and simply…I love you.

Where Only Love Goes

I was sitting here contemplating how each day that we're together, for you my love deepens. I was wondering what you had planned for this weekend, for all of the love you've sewn, it's time for some reaping. Possibly sitting on lush Savanna plains as mist morning dew seepens. Up on picnic blankets to celebrate this most joyest occasion. We can plot star constellations and road trip through each other's imagi-nation and sight see each other's soul and take pictures with our third eye lens and develop them with love. And nourish each other back to health with firm shoulder rubs.

That feeling you felt when we hugged...that's my heart's DJ bumping sound waves played to the tune of Miles Dave-n-Bustas like to run game, with metaphors that's lame, but I hope you're free this weekend to take a trip cross country on my Soul Train...cuz it's so plain to see that you are the one for me...and I hope you stay tuned...My Ori says Esu...you be Osun...you be my night light like full Moons...and I hope soon to make melodic tunes of our four part harmony—deep breaths, soft moans, candlelight flickers and my lips as they release from your...

Hips and I hope there is no fear. I say come close for round two is near. Please know my words are sincere when I say that your skin is as soft as cashmere. With these hands here, I explore new frontiers and now thickens the plot, you had my heart racing 40 nautical knots, to taste some of your warm butta scotch. And I've reserved a spot to make our night complete. On a four-day retreat in Aspen under Persian land sheets. Now let me unzip that Old Navy Fleece and release that tension with a full body deep tissue massage as incense aroma begins its ascension. As candle light flames aid your silhouette to dance amongst cabin partitions. I'm having private auditions for an all star cast of two. This is a role play and baby you be the star for the day. I be Tarzan, you be Jane. And when the drama begins, we won't need no stunt doubles. I can play King Kong walking on all fours with my bare knuckles. Your back and chest taste of honey suckle, warm caramel, vanilla bath bubbles, now let me unloosen that belt buckle...

Girl you know you So So, Def–tifying, with those chestnut, hazel eyes, and those succulent thick thighs and...damn...you make me feel like a kid in Showbiz. I just wanna be your summer, you can be my wiz-dom, and as we become in tune, with the sun, stars and moon, our hearts finds a groove, in perfect harmony with our spiritual aura, we bring in seasons like budding new flora—and in a state of amore I am—not afraid to profess it. You make time stop like Houston highways when congested. And if you haven't guessed it, gyal I'm digging you. On cosmic vibrations that's more than spiritual. And on this centennial, you have me wanting more. Have me speaking in tongues on some, En François, je t'adore. Or Por favor ¿Quieres casarte conmigo? As King Arthur is to medieval, you are a breath of fresh air. You see that north star, just close your eyes and let's go there...

As we walk on lotus petals, holding hands across moonlit lakes at the base of Kilimanjaro mountain peaks, I feel the heat from our Djembe heartbeats. We know God speaks in a language that only love can distinguish; between forever and temporary, dreamer or visionary, classic or contemporary, the one night stand, or the one to marry. You smell like sweet raspberry and juicy black cherries...man forget Jerry Springer: I'm Jerry Sprung on your...cosmic webpage, and your essence has been bookmarked – www – dot – she so angelic – dot – com (e) over to my place in a flash, so we can splash in champagne bubble baths, laugh and hone in on our craft of...creating universes...using these uni-verses and stanzas...

And this ain't no poet propaganda. This is just a man that's down and up for you, and with some luck or two, I can reserve a table for two– souls...And as the drama unfolds, and truth be told...I have two one-way tickets to a place where only love goes.

... a place where only love goes!

What Must I Do To Fulfill My Purpose?

The Garden Of Spitten

In the beginning
God created the heavens and the earth
And the earth was without form, and void
And darkness was upon the face of the deep
And the Spirit of God moved upon the face of the waters

And God said, "Let there be Poetry"
And there was Poetry
And Poetry began to multiply on the earth
And for a time, it was good
Poetry began to define, with rhythmic lines
That articulated the various experiences of mankind

And in due time
Poetry learned the art of divination
Learned how to change weather patterns with thought inclinations
And through medical palpations
Poetry taught Lucy how to walk upright
How to put ideas in a conceptual framework and recite
The fusion of words, metaphors, and adverbs
Chauffeured through a road map
In which they traveled to the depths of imagination
Where they greeted each other with a soul clap
    Of course on the side that's Black
    Where they could have the greatest impact

They lived in the midst of the Garden of Spitten
Where art was not painted, but written
And in the beginning, Poetry was in full submission

Facing reality and writing five times a day
On papyrus scrolls or tablets made of clay
And on one day, faster than the speed of Sunrays
God appeared to Poetry in the Garden

God said, "You may eat from every poet-tree
    but you must not abandon your roots"
He said, "You are made of trees
    and that you must bare fruit"
"This is an absolute," God declared to the herd
"You must use wisely this gift I've given you of the spoken word"

And in a manner of the birds, God flew off into the mountains
On their game, Poetry began recounting
All of the words of God that had been said
They vowed to the ancestors that they would not be misled

But that was too swiftly said
And now enters the serpent
His goal was to control and gather souls for purchase
And with the skill of the merchant he slithered by
    Poetry and proclaimed
"I have some shiny new gifts that you can obtain"
"If you follow my plan the world will be screaming your name"
"You just have to abandon where you came from"
"Cuz that style is old"
"This is how it's done now"
"So leave your roots in the cold"
"I can give you air time and put your face in magazines"
"You will obtain lots of money and across
    the world you'll be traveling"
"The only thing I ask before I make my ascendance"
"Is that you can say anything you want
    just avoid topics with substance"

And poetry was beguiled by the words spoken by the serpent
Poetry abandoned his roots and at first he was nervous
Poetry began to write poems that were not of its spirit

Poetry fell off because God's word he didn't fear it

And the Earth lapsed into the Poetic Dark Ages
No longer was new material written on the pages
No longer did Poetry produce sages
Poetry was now in a box and ideas lived in cages
To God's amazement he asked, "What has Poetry done?"
"How could Poetry do this to himself?
    Does he know where he came from?"
So he sent his son *Creativity* to show him how it's done

Creativity was the only begotten son
Only he could get Poetry out of the midst of the slum
And only he could remind Poetry where he came from

He reminded him of empires that once stood
    at the foot of civilization
How Harriet Tubman was a force for emancipation
How shell toe Addidas helped to defy gravitation
And how Poetry used to be the president of the Imagi-Nation
How Poetry used to get standing ovations
When he brought comfort to those with hearts aching
Then Poetry came to the realization that he had been hoodwinked
Bamboozled
Lead astray
Run amuck
Because of his desire to be heard instead of felt
    his poetry began to suck
But to his luck, God had favor
And granted Poetry another chance
And through this ordeal, Poetry's writing began to advance
And the crops began to grow in the minds of the people
No longer did Poetry **not** give his heart to the people
And Poetry began to bare fruit
All because the wisdom of Creativity brought him back to his roots
And it was all good!

Black People
Are Scared Of Heights

These are times of plagues, times of plagues I say
Times of trials and tribulations, times of trials I must say
Not plagues of the body, but plagues of the mind
We walk around with expensive watches, but we don't know the time
Most suffer throughout their life cuz they never fulfilled their dreams
Feeling they can't achieve because of low self-esteem
Looking at others do what seems to be impossible tasks
Can't foresee a thriving future, cuz they don't know their past
Don't know about their people and their thriving civilizations
How we created arts and sciences when there were no Caucasians
And what's really amazing and it seems so apparent
Is that these plagues are curable, just study your parent's parents
I'm a say what's wrong with Black people
I'm going to tell you tonight
The single biggest problem with Black folks
Is that Black folk are scared of heights

We wanna start record labels, and that seems to be a breeze
But we can't dig into the earth to find metals to make our own CDs
We work hard to make it to the NBA or win the Super Bowl
But can't fathom starting our own leagues, becoming CEOs
We make movies like *Soul Plane* and it's hard for me to take it
I want to see our *Lord of the Rings* and our trilogy to the *Matrix*
I don't think our worst problem here is hate, envy or greed
Black people can't move forward cuz we scared to succeed
We always complain about current radio compilations
But we scared to save up and build our own radio stations
We complain about high cell phone bills, paying extra for when we roam

But we won't learn the science of transmitting radio waves
    so we can build our own
We can't stand the government, but won't run for office
Won't start our businesses cuz we scared of the losses
We scared to leave the doctors to take back our health
Most men wonder why they can't keep their women
Cuz they unsure of they self
They don't display the confidence that they can do great things
They scared to struggle to see the joys life brings
Instead of northern birds, I wish our habits would go south
Instead of running behind great ideas, we'd rather run our mouth
About who's sleeping with who, or what she done did
How he flunked out of college, and she got so many kids
I speak about this topic because I feel the need to
Great minds discuss ideas, small minds discuss people
It's down right evil what people will say behind your back
But in your face they wanna smile, and give you a congrats
…On a job well done but I simply ignore it
They talk a hot game but have nothing to show for it
We can't speak greatness into existence because our thoughts are muffled
We can't *think* high enough to *look* beyond our troubles
I say this with sincerity
I speak with all my might
I boldly tell the congregation
I'm not scared of heights

I've migrated with birds from Utah to the Ghanges
I tight-roped along asteroid belts from here to Uranus
And on Saturn's rings is where my journey begins
With my eyes closed and arms open battling solar winds
And as the Earth spins counter clockwise on its axis
I walk barefoot in the desert squeezing wine from a cactus
With each new revelation I get, I make time stop
For fun, I play with my son, doing hopscotch on tree tops
I soar through hurricanes in a flash and I don't need a cape
I jump out of rocket ships so I can free fall from outer space
I go into deep meditation so I can plan my escape
I visit other galaxies so much I have Alien screw tapes

I'm about to take flight
I'm about to take flight
With a righteous *sho* you right
I'm not scared of heights

If you envision a world of which you surpass what the ancients did
There's only one thing to do Black People
And that's simply to think BIG!

Gravity

There are forces working in the universe to keep objects down
A secret mysterious force designed to keep all objects down
A force invisible to the eye
Even the nose can't catch its scent
Nor can the tongue savor its taste
Or the hands feel its torment
It has no origins, yet it expands the depths of the multi-verse
The more you struggle against it, the more it seems to get worse
It is a law of nature and it affects all of humanity
This force that I speak of is none other than gravity
It is stronger than electro magnetism
It is the force behind racism, sexism and classism
Fakism
Hatism
And terrorism
We no longer think in boxes, but prisms
Cuz we hate in 3D
And the light shown through the prism reveals our true colors
No longer do we have friends, comrades or brothers
For when you reach for new heights
They use the force of gravity to hold you down
They use every trick in the book to try and hold you down
And through this capacity
We find many forms of gravity
You know them better as:
Lust
Hate
Envy or

Jealousy
Many have learned how to harness the power of gravity at an early age
When another kid was doing well, they did something
   as not to be upstaged
They always want to be in the limelight
When you come out with a style, they are the first ones to bite
But since they can't do what you do better, they have
   to tear down your name
Hoping that if you fall, then they can get some fame
Always wondering what's going on in your life so they can critique
Talking about you behind your back
But smiling in your face when you meet
Two-faced individuals with no life of their own
You can tell because they're always talking about
   someone else's life on the phone
They can't accept that you're happy and in your life there's peace
So they use gravity on you like misguided voodoo priests
They probably got a hold of one of your hair follicles
Created a doll in your likeness, and don't think it's not possible
Because I've seen it done
They do it all of the time where I come from
If you get a raise at your job, they say you don't deserve it
If you get an award from your community, they say you didn't earn it
If you end up with a beautiful woman, they wonder how'd you do that
If someone says you are very intelligent, they say he's not all that!
It's really a sad story when you look at their life
No talents, no ambitions, no purpose in life
Malcolm X lost his life to gravity
Marcus Garvey was deported due to gravity
Able was slain by his brother Cain cuz of gravity
Countless careers have been short-lived because of this travesty
See misery likes company, so don't let it get to you
When you feel the force of gravity just do what I do
Step out in the middle of the storm on any given Sunday
Plant both feet into the water and use the ocean as your runway
Start hummin and summon the spirit of Harriet Tubman
And keep running until you hear the ancestors drumming
Pick up speed at 360 nautical thoughts per second

Turn on your 3rd eye lens to increase your perception
The more spirits you summon, the merrier
And keep on stepping until you break the sound barrier
Then lift your legs up and let the force help you to break free
The force of truth is stronger than the force of gravity
Just stay focused on what's to come
Step on oxygen molecules charting a course towards the sun
Stepping over airplanes, vultures, and hawks
Piercing through nimbus clouds causing rain to fall as you walk
And transform into a sentient being and
Poke a hole in the ozone layer
Leave the atmosphere
With the words of sacred prayers
Because at times, most fear what they can't see
What they can't understand
What they can be
So to break free from the force of gravity
You must merge with the sun and let your light shine
Cuz there's nothing that can hold you down when
    you're one with the divine

Peace!

Emotion And Reflection: Key Components For A Rite Of Passage

There have been numerous discussions on various African rites of passage experiences throughout time. With the longing for a sense of self and history, African-Americans have been struggling on how best to implement a rites of passage program here in the United States that is relevant and meaningful in the lives of African-American youth and adults. Most traditional African cultures participate in a rites of passage program of some sort. It serves as a way to mark significant milestones in one's life, teaches initiates the proper use of power, tests them on courage and leadership, reveals secrets on the male/female relationship and how it relates to the governance of the universe, instructs them on community living, teaches them about the history of their people, teaches them their roles and responsibilities towards family and the corporate community, and educates them on the secrets of nature and how to use it to their advantage.

Much literature has been written on African rites of passage and this will not be a rehash of what has been so eloquently articulated by various authors. I have supplied some suggested reading at the end of this article.

What I want to discuss here are the psychological aspects of a rites of passage program and the area not often talked about when discussing the benefits of such a program: a means to create experiences for self-reflection. A deeper look into the nature of a rites of passage program reveals a method that brings about greater meaning for rituals as these are used to facilitate the process of reflection, which is a major component of spiritual growth for human beings. "Truth" cannot be told, only experienced. A rite of passage, within a controlled environment, constructs a micro social matrix that creates the circumstances necessary for the initiate to experience certain realities, which if successfully completed at this stage will yield tremendous social benefits, not only for him/herself, but for the community at large. A rite of passage brings about an array of emotions through the rigorous nature of the rituals, which aids in long-term memory, and which uses these events as spiritual time stamps for points of self-reflection. I will veer off a little bit and speak on the nature of reflection before I delve into emotions, what it is and how it relates to this topic.

The Nature of the Universe: Reflection

In the African traditional sense, "God," in the beginning, in its perfection, at some point realized it was imperfect because it had no means of experiencing itself. In the beginning there were no concepts at all, just a oneness. So "it" created this "matrix" called the "universe" so it could have a "place" to have experiences—so in essence, "it" could get to know who "it" is (as knowledge is based on experience).

A feature that makes this universe unique, in comparison to how it was in the "beginning (according to African wisdom), is its ability to send and receive feedback between objects (concepts). It's kind of hard to "visualize" a state where there are no conceptions of any kind. This was not an easy task for our ancestors as well, so they used the color black to symbolize this oneness. The color black represents undifferentiated existence from which all things come into being. We are able to perceive "objects" in this "blackness" because of light. We are able to see and perceive those things because light reflects or refracts off of these objects and informs the consciousness of its current state, texture, density, etc. Our safe navigation in this reality is based upon this system of reflection and feedback.

Reflection aids the process of feedback. Feedback was the missing component in the "beginning" and is the reason why the supreme creative force could not experience itself: it could not "see." Every system we can think of is in a state of transformation. In this constant state of transformation there are inputs and outputs. The inputs are the result of the environment's influence on the system, and the outputs are the influence of the system on the environment. What separates inputs and outputs is duration of time, as in before and after, past and present.

During this process, information about the result of the transformation process, or an action (whatever it may be) is sent back as input data (information) to the input system. In other words, the input system does something to cause a change in the environment. The result of that change is therefore sent back to the input system as information and that information is interpreted by the input system (given meaning). So YOU (input system) throw a rock in the river (output) and the water ripples in the river as a result (transformation). YOU are able to perceive this process because the light from the sun reflects off of the objects and you are able to perceive its transformation. However, sight is not the only way we receive feedback. In this case, the sound from the rock hitting the water would be a form of feedback as well. The result of you throwing the rock in the water is sent back to the brain and is interpreted as "water rippling." We are able to judge, perceive, make decisions, etc., based upon this system of feedback. Without feedback there would be no existence: you wouldn't know transformation was occurring.

All of the world's economic markets are based on consumer feedback. If something costs too much, people don't buy it. If an item is fairly cheap, people buy it more abundantly. Prices on items allow for consumer feedback on the worth of an item. You have negative and positive feedback. Positive feedback leads to divergent behavior: an explosion or expansion of a system. Each plus is followed by another plus which starts a snowball effect. The examples are numerous: chain reaction, population explosion, industrial expansion, capital invested at compound interest, inflation, proliferation of cancer cells, etc. A positive feedback loop ultimately leads to the system destroying itself, either through explosion or blocking of its functions.

A system maintains balance by the introduction of negative feedback loops (Set, Satan). Negative feedback is necessary to keep all things in balance. This is why we have thunderstorms, earthquakes, crime, death, volcanic eruptions, droughts, accidents, etc. This is an attempt by the universe to make its creation always strive to continue life and form new things (be in a perpetual state of becoming, which makes evolution a fact). If a system becomes too comfortable and sees no reason for change, it dies and creation comes to a stand still. This is the secret behind the biblical Genesis story of Adam and Eve. If Satan didn't come in and disrupt them in their "perfection," they (symbolized by Adam and Eve) would have eventually stopped creation as they would not be in a continual stage of learning, of becoming, of internal transformation. On a more personal level, any of us who has been in an intimate relationship with someone knows that if there is no change in the relationship (no fluctuations in activities), the relationship dies. People get bored with repetition. If the two people involved in the relationship are not growing, they are not reaching for higher heights, and then the relationship ceases to exist. We seek excitement, we seek change (the biblical story of the Israelites complaining about the manna should come to mind). Negative feedback leads to adaptive or goal-seeking behavior. In a negative loop every variation toward a plus triggers a correction toward the minus, and vice versa. Energy (life) therefore oscillates between positive and negative polarities and is working towards an equilibrium it will never obtain. You do not want to be in a state of equilibrium because equilibrium equals death: perfection, flat line.

This is why initiates are given hardships to overcome in a rites of passage program. It is a ritual allegory for the feedback laws of nature and how hardships are actually mechanisms put in place by the creator to maintain balance and to keep us seeking equilibrium (although never attainable). These hardships keep human beings (and life in general) in a constant state of becoming, a constant state of trying to be something better than we were yesterday. This is realized through self-reflection on events, which is a result of feedback sent to the brain. This is the underlying functioning of a rite of passage and we will see below how emotions facilitate this process of self-reflection, which ultimately allows us to give meaning to life itself.

The importance of emotions and long-term memory

Recent studies have shed light on how emotions help us to remember certain events in our lives. The importance of memory is key to self-reflection, which is one of the main goals of a rite of passage program. Here are some key points to consider when thinking about the effects of emotions:

• Emotionally charged events are remembered better.
• Pleasant emotions are usually remembered better than unpleasant ones.
• Positive memories contain more contextual details (which in turn, helps memory).
• Strong emotion can impair memory for less emotional events and information experienced at the same time.
• It's the emotional arousal, not the importance of the information, that helps memory.

In other words, what we store in long-term memory depends on how we were affected emotionally by the event. More than likely you do not remember the last time a fly flew by your face. The appearance of a fly did not arouse any strong emotions in you, so the event is rendered insignificant. However, if a Bangle tiger were to chase you down a street, the strong sense of fear would most definitely catapult this occurrence to the forefront of your mind, and you would likely remember the event throughout your life.

Another aspect of emotions is mood. Essentially, what is noticed and encoded in our psyche is dependant upon two effects of mood:

Mood Congruence: Here we remember events that match our current mood (thus, when we're depressed, we tend to remember negative events).

Mood Dependence: This refers to the fact that remembering is easier when your mood at retrieval matches your mood at encoding (thus, your chances of remembering an event or fact are greater if you evoke the emotional state you were in at the time of experiencing the event or learning the fact) .

In other words, I am more apt to remember an event if I am currently in the emotional state that matches the event I am trying to remember. For example, if I just broke up with my girlfriend, I feel a sense of loss and depression (depending if I really liked her or not). Because of this breakup, I might remember events such as me losing a friend in a car accident or me losing a job. This would be an example of mood congruence. Mood dependence, to me, is a conscious evoking of an emotion in an effort to retrieve a memory. We do this unconsciously with songs we are trying to remember. We try to put ourselves at the place we heard the song and conjure up the emotions of the song in order to remember the lyrics.

Conclusion

How does all of this relate and what do emotions and memory have to do with African rites of passage programs? A rites of passage program stirs up strong emotions through the rigorous obstacles an initiate has to overcome during this development. The initiate, later on in life, can use these experiences to go back and retrieve solutions to current problems (Sankofa). If an initiate was required to be courageous and hunt a rhino, then that same courage might be needed in the face of an external enemy trying to take over his/her community's land. That same courage will be needed in the political arena when trying to pass laws for the betterment of society against those who want to maintain the status quo, or when trying to clean up urban neighborhoods from drugs, prostitution, police brutality or even regentrification.

The key component of spiritual development is predicated on one's ability to reflect on life and give meaning to events. We come to the realizations of certain truths when we have time to sit back and think about them deeply. What information is being reflected back at us? What does it all mean? A rite of passage puts a time stamp on events, which makes it easier for the brain to retrieve memories for self-reflection. We remember things to look for solutions to current problems. This process we call "rites" prints these memories on our consciousness for easy retrieval if we are in the same emotional state as the initial event, so we can remember how we solved similar problems when we were in a more concentrated and controlled environment.

A rite of passage is a process that teaches conflict management: a method to seek balance. The negative inputs in our lives serve as components to help us grow spiritually. The universe is designed to send and receive feedback between objects (to make itself aware of its current condition). Our ability to see objects and perceive their transformation is dependent on the light that is reflected back at us—the same with our spiritual state and spiritual transformation. It is through deep self-reflection (our internal light of truth) that we are able to perceive the deeper truths of past events and to gain insight to possible meanings of those events, and to learn about ourselves and what must be done to improve ourselves.

If we believe the traditional African world view on why "God" created this universe, then we can see the importance of self-reflection in "God's" development. Reflection and feedback are laws of nature that helps the supreme creative intelligence to get to know itself, and since we (ba'ntu, human beings) are the nervous system of the creator, it is our job to send messages to it to inform it on the state of affairs on this plane. We do this through positive/negative affirmations, prayers, and rituals. Most spiritual systems proclaim that "God" is omnipresent. If so, then we are nothing but aspects of the creator and when we do rituals and prayers, we are in essence holding conversations with ourselves, informing ourselves of our current condition, using power to control our destiny and trying to make sense of our conditions.

To exist is to be on a perpetual mission to find meaning in this reality. Whether that meaning is predetermined or given meaning by mankind is another discussion all together. But a rite of passage allows us to recreate the laws of nature in our social environment so that we may experience an array of emotions that will ultimately serve as mnemonic devices that cause us to reflect and bring meaning to our lives. We grow as spirits when we understand what is and why. Why is our source of power. Without it, we are powerless (notes from the Matrix Reloaded). The process of a rite of passage goes beyond simply keeping tradition alive: it is one solution that fosters a spirit of triumph, conflict management, spiritual growth through reflection and social cohesiveness. This is a component not often talked about when discussing rites of passage programs and I think this process needs to be explored more deeply in order for humanity to better reap its benefits.

References:

Web
Feedback - http://pespmc1.vub.ac.be/FEEDBACK.html
Reflection - http://en.wikipedia.org/wiki/Reflection%28physics%29
Rites of passage - http://www.ritesofpassage.org/

Emotions and Memory
Anderson, A.K. & Phelps, E.A. 2001. Lesions of the human amygdala impair enhanced perception of emotionally salient events. *Nature*, 411, 305-309.
Canli, T., Desmond, J.E., Zhao, Z. & Gabrieli, J.D.E. 2002. Sex differences in the neural basis of emotional memories. Proceedings of the National Academy of Sciences, 99, 10789-10794.
Charles, S.T., Mather, M. & Carstensen, L.L. 2003. Aging and Emotional Memory: The Forgettable Nature of Negative Images for Older Adults. *Journal of Experimental Psychology*: General, 132(2), 310-24.
D'Argembeau, A., Comblain, C. & Van der Linden, M. 2002. Phenomenal characteristics of autobiographical memories for positive, negative, and neutral events. *Applied Cognitive Psychology*, 17(3), 281-94.
Erk, S. et al. 2003. Emotional context modulates subsequent memory effect. *Neuroimage*, 18, 439-447.
Fletcher, P.C., Anderson, J.M., Shanks, D.R., Honey, R., Carpenter, T.A., Donovan, T., Papadakis, N. & Bullmore, E.T. (2001). Responses of

human frontal cortex to surprising
events are predicted by formal associative learning theory. *Nature Neuroscience*, 4, 1043
1048.

Gray, J.R., Braver, T.S. & Raichle, M.E. Integration of emotion and cognition in the lateral prefrontal cortex. Proceedings of the National Academy of Sciences, 99, 4115-4120.
Hamann, S. 2001. Cognitive and neural mechanisms of emotional memory. *Trends in Cognitive Sciences*, 5 (9), 394-400.

Lewis, P.A. & Critchley, H.D. 2003. Mood-dependent memory. *Trends in Cognitive Sciences*, 7 (9).

Lupien, S.J., Gaudreau, S., Tchiteya, B.M., Maheu, F., Sharma, S., Nair, N.P.V., Hauger, R.L., McEwen, B.S. & Meaney, M.J. 1997. Stress Induced Declarative Memory Impairment in Healthy Elderly Subjects: Relationship to Cortisol Reactivity. *The Journal of Clinical Endocrinology & Metabolism*, 82 (7), 2070-2075.

Nielson, K.A., Yee, D. & Erickson, K.I. 2002. Modulation of memory sto age processes by post-training emotional arousal from a semantically unrelated source. Paper presented at the Society for Neuroscience annual meeting in Orlando, Florida, 4 November.

Nijholt, I., Farchi, N., Kye, M-J., Sklan, E.H., Shoham, S., Verbeure, B., Owen, D., Hochner, B., Spiess, J., Soreq, H. & Blank, T. 2003. Stress-induced alternative splicing of acetylcholinesterase results in enhanced fear memory and long-term potentiation. *Molecular Psychiatry* advance online publication, 28 October 2003.

Richards, J.M. & Gross, J.J. (2000). Emotion Regulation and Memory: The Cognitive Costs of Keeping One's Cool. Journal of Personality and Social Psychology, 79 (3), 410-424.

Richeson, J. & Shelton, N. 2003. When Prejudice Does Not Pay: Effects of Interracial Contact on Executive Function. Psychological Science, 14(3).

Sacchetti, B., Baldi, E., Lorenzini, C.A. & Bucherelli, C. 2002. Cerebellar role in fear conditioning consolidation. Proc. Natl. Acad. Sci. U.S.A., 99 (12), 8406-8411.

Strange, B.A., Hurleman, R. & Dolan, R.J. In press. An emotion-induced retrograde amnesia in humans is amygdala and b-adrenergic dependent. Proceedings of the National Academy of Sciences.

Stuss, D.T., Binns, M.A., Murphy, K.J. & Alexander, M.P. 2002.
    Dissociations Within the Anterior Attentional System: Effects of
    Task Complexity and Irrelevant Information on
    Reaction-Time Speed and Accuracy. Neuropsychology, 16 (4), 500–513.

Walker, W.R., Skowronski, J.J. & Thompson, C.P. 2003. Life Is Pleasant —
    and Memory Helps to Keep It That Way! Review of General
    Psychology, 7(2),203-10.

Yamasaki, H., LaBar, K.S. & McCarthy, G. Dissociable prefrontal brain
    systems for attention and emotion. Proc. Natl. Acad. Sci. USA,
    99(17), 11447-51.

Suggested Readings:

Africanism in American Culture (1990). Joseph E. Holloway.

A Peculiar People: Slave Religion and Community-Culture Among the Gullahs
    (1988). Margaret Creel

The Four Moments of the Sun (1981) and

Flash of the Spirit (1983). Robert Farris Thompson

The African Presence in Black America, Jacob U. Gordon

African Religions and Philosophy. (1969). John S. Mbiti,

Kawaida Theory. (1980). Maulana Karenga

The Journey: Adolescent Rites of Passage (1998). Paul Hill, Jr.

COMING OF AGE: African American Male Rites of Passage, Paul Hill, Jr.

The Importance of Ritual to Children. (unpublished dissertation) (1994).
    Deanna Dorsa

Mythography: The Study of Myths and Rituals. (1986). William G Doty

What Are You Doing?

There are too many people with opinions
But few who actually know what they talk about
Always some know-it-all behind internet chat rooms
Who got something to say about education, but hasn't stepped foot
    in a classroom
Always want to preach about what the church ain't about
But don't feed homeless people to show them what compassion's about
See, I always wonder about folks who got something to say but little to add
By sacrificing their time for a cause instead of commenting about
    the aftermath
Our children's future is up for grabs
But we can't build solid foundations because there are
    too many Afro imitations acting like crabs
Pulling down people who are in the business of doing
While they just come home from work
    and watch the television, gum chewing
Lip spewing
About opinions they formulated watching from the sidelines
Secretly wanting to step into the game, but haven't read the guidelines
And for some time we all must all be on our grind
But some won't step up to the plate because they on some
    "shit, I got mines"

    See
I am because we are
And if we ain't
Then who am I?

    Who am I to say that teachers aren't teaching nothing

If I don't volunteer to help teachers after school or something?
Who am I to talk about politicians not being the voice of the people
If I don't go to the town hall meetings to bring suggestions to the people?
Who am I to talk about the best approach to raising children
When I don't have any seeds to talk from experience for
     community building?
The people who do the least, do the most talking
I swear they are a part of the Crip gang
Cuz when it's time to do the work
It's them I C-Walking
I've walked through the hearts of men
And I see the writings on the wall
I've seen the desolate minds of our fathers
Because our elders dropped the ball
Before you walk, you must crawl
Before you can communicate
You must call
And we call on all of ya'll to volunteer your time
Because we sho-nuff are running out of...time
But if you choose not to help, then move out of the way of the ones
     who are doing
Go back home after work and continue to watch TV, gum chewing
Let the people who are in the business of doing make their mistakes
And if you aren't in the business of doing, then who are you to critique?
Too busy worried about who you're doing instead of what you're doing.
While you sit idle in your circles, there are people in the streets moving
Upset at people who can't make it to all of the personal party gatherings
They can't because they too busy in the libraries gathering
Information for better strategies to implement with the insight
     they've been gathering
To go back into the community and build with community leaders in
     private gatherings
So they can in turn go out to ghetto fields and plant seeds and nourish
     young minds and sit back and wait for the right season to start gathering
Everybody doesn't have to fight the same battles
Just be about something
Use your life to fight and right the wrongs
Whether it's through legislation or through song

With ideology from Odu Ifa, or through psalms
Whether you read Iwe Pele, or read palms
As long as the Republicans drop bombs and pregnant mothers shoot
   needles through arms
We all should be up in arms fighting for healthcare for veterans who suffer
   from diseases from Desert Storm.
A father mourns the loss of another son gone
A fan mourns the death of Hip Hop music now gone
A community mourns the loss of leadership now gone
Word ain't bond when you talk more than you are doing
While you sit there unintellectualizing about what someone else is doing
Our community's social fabric stands to lay in ruins
All I'm saying is, be about something
Because if we don't stand for something
All of our soldiers would have fallen for nothing

Pay-Write

Most poets feel a creative urge and free write. But I choose to charge readers, despite their ability to pay—attention or ability to convey, their thoughts to show they have some level of comprehension. Nothing in life is free. It's gonna cost you a brain cell to journey with me. So hurry with me, at least 20,000 leagues under the sea—as we swim in a fan-ta–sea. And if you Seaweed… just swim past the smoke filled paragraphs and proceed to the subterranean toll booth and pay the fare. Our ancestors paid with their lives, so it's worth the cost dear. With no fear, I enter the land of imagination. Where turtles come with bullet proof shells and poetry is a high-paying occupation. Where clouds drip starburst flavored raindrops. And where MOCHA flavored coffee flows from Ethiopian hill tops. A place where people walked backwards everywhere they went. And a place where righteous elders ran the government, while hippy haired youth played Parliament.

Where Atomic Que Dogs hopped around college parties, and poets were as deep as Bob Marley and white boys stayed gnarly and people who wore locks were all Rasta – far – e…Eye's — see with 360/360 degree vision. With the ability to see subatomic particles and witness two cells in mid collision form another lifeform. I hope you brought your umbrella…it's gonna be another brainstorm. So hurry Cane…Abel's bout to offer his offerings. Only bring your best this time and witness what compassion brings. As sure as Saturn's rings rotate, let's set our own Plan so we can Net worth more than our current poor state. I write for all the unborn poets who are going to go through writer's block. I write for current poets whose forefathers lost their heritage on an auction block. I write for hidden poets who have yet to discover themselves and their God given ability. I write this pay write for all unsigned playwrights who survive on hope and agility.
Wasn't it worth the cost of the journey? Peace!

Free-Write

As time approaches, I arrive like the infant Joseph, in a lotus position trying to keep focus. In a bed of roses, I inhale incense smoke with cedar wooden holders. I astro-plane to the time of Zinjantropus. I arrive at a period that predates Moses, the Passover and the plague of locusts. I enter an alternate state of psychosis, taking Ritalin in small doses, while God exposes all the secrets of creation and what the spirit is composed of. As oxygen seeps in through the noses, I enter a realm of dead ancestors and classical music composers, as the flesh decomposes, the spirit rises above the ozone, it's

Time for evolution
no time for web browsing
It's time for restitution
You know it's time to move mountains
It's time to build institutions so we can know what living is

People fear time is running out, but time feared the pyramids. On my yearly pilgrimage, I take notes to combat the sacrilege from Mary Lefkowitz and all her constituents. I'm disappointed in the Masons and the Jesuits. I record the measurements from the Karnak monuments, to dead arguments about the Egyptian apocalypse and the alleged Exodus. I travel through celestial highways with no luggage, with no passport, dodging space rubbish. At the first signs of ruckus, I transform into a light beam and travel through the atmosphere at warp speed through the North Atlantic Jet Stream...about 20,000 leagues above the sea, I undergo a metamorphosis, radio waves bounce off me like satellites in orbit. As high as the hawk gets, I see clearly through the eyes of Heru. I can see Roman characters spelling out names in your alphabet soup.

It's time for a new tribe of apostles. I arrive in Cairo and leave out with Dead Sea Gospels. From Atlanta to Damascus, from Atlantis to Nazareth, I've traveled the globe with no hot air balloon or space probe. I redirect sound from the earlobes to go touch the garment of Christ's robe and come back and decipher the book of Job. I move like Jet Li in Hero, but use it for the benefit of my people.

I'm a word-smith, I pound out words on anvils, to make my words razor sharp to put opposition at a stand still. In desert landfills, I come up with my philosophies. I write poems in calligraphy to hide divine prophecies. In Egyptian typography and iconography, I capture the essence of the human spirit like a camera to photography. As long as it makes sense logically, I'll use ancient hypotheses to bring out the God in me.

Think Big

I often sit and wonder just how much of our (Africans in America) current condition is caused by our actions and goals in life. I will tell you up front that I know of our historical past, more than most would care to research, and the effects of colonialism and how the devastation impacted the people from the continent of Africa. So I am aware that we have had much to overcome. But I am still disappointed when I have discussions with my people when it comes to their aspirations and dreams. I have noticed that most people's goals and aspirations are, to put it plainly, mediocre. They have the ambition for something more, but the motivation and will to carry it out seems to be absent.

I am not saying that in comparison to me they lag behind, but when I mention the little things I have done in the past, they get excited like it was the biggest thing in the world. When I ask them if they're serious, they often reply, "Wish I could do something like that." I am a firm believer that we are the manifestation of "God" and that he/she/it gave us the qualities and skills necessary to do "God" like things. Our Kemetic ancestors believed this wholeheartedly and this is one of the reasons they became the "society of legacy" we so admire today. In other words, they thought big. They thought of something and had the big picture in mind and executed their visions. It was culture to master yourself and strive to be like the ones who dwelt in the heavens. That meant that you had to think beyond your perceived worldly limitations.

I look at how Europeans operate in the world. Don't get me wrong, I believe they could do a whole bunch to improve relations with the earth's occupants and the natural environment, but you have to admire the level of aspiration they as a whole have and the goal setting they put in place for themselves. It appears that Africans in America will never reach the level of our counterparts because collectively we do not aspire for the largest of goals. This is partly because we would have to become what we hate to obtain what Europeans has been able to accumulate over the years.

When the Pope gave the okay to enslave Africans because they didn't have any "souls" (which puzzles me since we are the ones they come to when they need soul in their music and religious services), Europeans designed a plan that spanned several hundred years. They actually developed plans for how their children were going to continue slavery and how they were going to keep Africans subjugated so they could continue to prosper on their wealth building initiative. We are living at the height of their plan. America is the richest nation on Earth and White people rule every aspect of its being. They control the laws, imports, exports, manufacturing, the religion, the military, the value of goods, the distribution of wealth, the press, the security, the family structure, what's hot, what's not, the image of beauty, the language, the technology, and even all of the above in other countries. I will do an article later on the power structure of the Jesuits, Masons and Nights Templar, so you can get a better understanding of the organization's goals and methods of operations.

When I talk to my people, they do not want to control any of the above mentioned aspects of this society. They just want to make it to the level where they can be validated by Europeans. I speak to Hip Hop artists and poets about their plans. They just want to make a couple of albums and go platinum. Why don't they want to own a true record label, some radio stations, and manufacture CDs? Puff Daddy talks a good game, but he has to renegotiate his record management company ever few years. Bad Boy is not a true record company; it is a management firm. All of America's sports talent is comprised of Africans. These Africans do not strive to build their own league; they just want to make it in the NBA and get a ring and some endorsements. The only reason Jackie Robinson was accepted into the National Baseball League is because the Negro League was making too much money on its own and threatened the NBL's market share (not to mention all the real talent was in the Negro Leagues). What better way to dismantle a people's ability to grow independently than to integrate them?

Oprah Winfrey once had a show in which she was granting the wishes of people who sent in letters of some sort. To her dismay, she found that most people requested that she pay their bills or pay for them to go on a vacation. She said that while she was happy to pay for all of those things, she was disappointed that the majority of the people's desires were so mediocre. She said no one asked her to help them start an enterprise and that she would have been ready and willing to help fund it.

This is why true education needs to be the focal point within our culture. It allows us to obtain power. Power is the ability to influence the environment consistent with one's self-interest. Education allows an individual or society to be effective in gaining independent mastery of this power of influence. The slave here in America was removed from the effective negotiation of his/her skills because their skills belonged to someone else: the slave master (Akbar, 1998). Neo Slavery has given Africans in America the opportunity to spend a decade in training beyond secondary school, and can only develop skills that permit their masters (Corporate America) to negotiate a trade. You have brilliant CPAs who cannot see past working for a big firm, doctors who can't see past working for an HMO, and intelligent athletes who can't see beyond getting a ring and a trophy. You have leaders in Black organizations who can't conceive a town in their city in which Black people run the politics and the distribution of resources in their own neighborhoods.

A slave living in Canada by the name of George Ross was interviewed in 1863 and said, concerning the mentality of some of the head slaves, that "For instance…their masters send them to mill and give them a little money and tell them, 'You are a good boy, and we will give you enough to eat, drink, and clothe you pretty well and you should make yourself satisfied.' …Undoubtedly, they keep others from going by saying, 'You see what privileges we have, and if you do as well as we do, your master will treat you well, and here is a home for you'" (Blassingame 1977: 407).

This mentality, sad to say, still exists within the majority of African Americans. Not saying all people are meant to be entrepreneurs, but our ambitions should go well beyond working for some large company that's not black-owned, getting a nice house, some new shoes, our hair done every week, going to the hottest party, copping jewelry, having wheels that spin, getting a record deal, paying bills, and finding a man or woman, etc.

We should be able to think beyond the physical realm and build on the inner temple that will enable us to achieve big things. If our ancestors could do it, I am pretty sure we are equipped with the necessary tools to do big things also. Now, I'm not taking away from the accomplishments of the Civil Rights Movement, but the people didn't have the ultimate goal in mind. The objective was assimilation. Studies prove that blacks had more when they were segregated and did more business with each other. The reason we still have the problems we see today is because Blacks then and now can't see past civil rights.

In order to be a true nation you must have these four elements: land, a military, a government, and the nation must be an exporter of goods and services. If one of these elements is missing, you are not a nation. In order to export goods and services you need land to manufacture it. In order to regulate the distribution of the land and its resources you must have a governmental body in place that sets national policy. And just in case you are invaded by foreign powers, you need a way to defend yourself, thus the military. I should add one more element—this same nation must be in control of the education of the people. My people are destroyed for a lack of knowledge (Hosea 4:6). It is time we think big, black people. If we are at the bottom, there is no other place to go but up.

References

Blassingame, John W. (1977) *Slave Testimony*, Louisiana Sate University Press

Akbar, Naim. (1998). *Know Thyself*, Mind Productions & Associates, Inc.

Random Poems

I don't spit poetry to move crowds
But to move mountains
To make time stop and make people think
Let the words sink into the minds
Like pages do with ink
And bring form to possibilities
And let these inventions become the community's medicine
Cuz we all in need of healing
from our Cultural Immune Deficiency Syndrome

****

My love is as deep as a Psalms
written by the hands of God herself
Your beauty is as radiant as the reflection of God herself
I feel electrical impulses when my fingertips
caress the cuticles of your afro
Every time I feel her smile over the phone, my soul glows
And lord knows, when I first met her, in my mind
her vibe left an imprint
her radiance is so bright that she makes the sun squint

****

My tongue moves with grace across your chest, doing figure
eights around your nipples while you moan and take deep breaths.
My arms cuffed behind you while my hands firmly grasp your
shoulders. Your neck tilted back slightly and your body
temperature is getting warmer. We've been waiting for months

and your body language speaks and says you're ready. At the speed of
passion I flip you over while African drums
thunder like Tommy in Belly.

****

....yeah, I remember that
Ooh oooh! Remember when we used to sneak into the movies while
ya girl distracted the ticket master? Remember how we used to walk
the country side at night and rename star constellations? Remember
when we used to meditate together back to back and our breaths were
in sync? Our thoughts were in sync and our hearts moved to the
rhythm of planetary heartbeats while Beat Street provided the
silhouette on the walls. I couldn't wait for our Morris days, and
as I took a look at the Time, it was 40 years later
and the marriage is still going strong

That Newly Wed Love! Mayen hold-up....bring dat back!

****

Who can move faster than a speeding bullet
running backwards on his hands?
Who can capsize mountain tops into tree trunk stumps
on the borders of Sudan?

The Black Lotus!

Who can reduce his frame to the size of an atom?
And play kickball with electrons and use
colored photons to make kinte patterns?

The Black Lotus!

Who can walk on lava and build pyramids in the center of the Earth?
Who can play hop scotch on continents
and reverse the rotation of the Earth?

The Black Lotus!
Who?
The Black Lotus!

The Black Lotus!

Who?

****

I built massive stone structures to pay homage to
God in *Monopotapa*
And noticed a dwarf star next to *Sirius A* and used its energy to light
up temples something proper
I studied with the Dagara and jumped over trees with the *Massai*
I jumped into my *Mada-gas-Car* and drove up to *Songhai*
I didn't want to *Kil-a-mon*, but *Jaro* be trippin
I *converse* with Hippos along the Nile while elephants be sippin
water that ran down the *Ethiopian* highlands
then run cross country through *Sahara* desert dry lands
Only to swing from trees in the central *Congo* rain forest
where our ancestors were first introduced to Osiris and his son Horus

****

The key to understanding God is to check its artistry
all things reflect thought concepts, so pardon me
If I dig a little deeper into nature and its intricacies
every time I look at the inside of a plant I get an epiphany
It's one harmonic symphony of codes and information
which reveals a method for my emancipation
There is no separation of matter and spirit
I think I found God in the study of quantum physics

****

We exchange histories as our lips hug
Lightly applying pressure to moist, soft symbols of real love

That speak sounds that vibrates to one's soul
Right hand down shirt, true feelings and curiosities unfold
and truth be told, she tastes like caramel sweet butterscotch
She "uhhh's" with vigor and now thickens the plot

****

We are in a state of emergency
I wish shallow persons could emerge and see
The deeper aspects of life
The secrets of nature
How there's nothing new under the sun
One, because we are all one
And only change form
Only change the perceptions of reality
There is an underlying essence behind the formalities
And in actuality we are just beacons of light
Traveling spoiled milky ways with divine hindsight
And as sparks ignite, I divine to ancestors to pray homage
Our people are still being destroyed for a lack of knowledge
That's why I am declaring a state of emergency
I wish shallow individuals could emerge and see
That no matter how grand it may seem
it's the middle where we must meet
Cuz in actuality, it's not all that deep

****

My clothes are soaking wet from running through brain storms
Every thunder clap is my signal to change form
Transform
Like optimus PRIME
Like McGruff
I sit back and take a bite of out CRIME
and now it's on kid
I write in a vast field of orchids
Undergo a metamorphosis
I'm in love with my poetry, she's gorgeous

Meditate in a deep forest
Animal life plays the riddim, the trees sings the chorus
I bust through cold ice stairs
and stay focused
poetry's known to grow chest hair
The Black Lotus
I can He He How like Missy
But when I Roar like a Grizzly, they say damn he gets busy
YES YES YA'LL

The Domestication Of The Negro

"How could so few white people rule so many black people? This is the thing you should want to know…The white man today will tell you that thousands of years ago, the black man in Africa was living in palaces; the black man was wearing silk; the black man in Africa was cooking and seasoning his food; the black man in Africa had mastered the arts and sciences. He knew the course of the stars in the universe before the man up in Europe knew that the earth wasn't flat. Is that right or wrong?"

I first heard the quote above in one of my early Africana Studies classes while watching a 1994 PBS film titled Malcolm X: Make It Plain (http://www.pbs.org/wgbh/amex/malcolmx/). The first line of questioning had such a profound impact on me that it literally changed the course of my studies, so much that I minored in it.

I often wondered how the European people were able to steal so many African people over such a long period of time. I was informed that the Europeans attempted to enslave the indigenous people of the "New World," but their efforts were futile (they ultimately resorted to genocide instead). Why then were they so unsuccessful with the indigenous people of what is now called America, but so successful with us? What was it about African people that made them such "good" slaves as opposed to other people on the earth? What was it about our mindset, our culture, that would allow more than 30 Million human beings to become enslaved and transported across the world? But more importantly, what was it going to take for us NOT to be enslaved again?

A possible answer came to me while I was watching a PBS special (got to love PBS) titled Guns, Germs and Steel (based on the book by the same title by Jared Diamond). Part of the discussion centered on the domestication of the cow, and what the criteria were for the domestication of animals in general. According to Diamond, there have only been 14 mammals that man has been able to successfully domesticate, and in the film they name four major characteristics needed for domestication: size, temperament/pleasant disposition, growth rate and diet. The Australian Broadcast System (ABC) had a similar   program   called   The   Animal   Attraction (http://abc.net.au/animals/program2/factsheet1.htm) and it adds to the equation: happy to breed in captivity, unlikely to panic, and social hierarchy.

After watching the program, I noticed that a lot of the characteristics shared among domesticated animals were also shared among indigenous African cultures. I wondered could this possibly be one of the major reasons why so many of us were enslaved. Could the answers lie in this PBS program? A quick summary will help to make things clearer for this discussion; I will only talk about the most relevant characteristics. NOTE: We will not examine the role Arabs, Jews or Africans played in the slave trade. That is beyond the scope of this article. We will focus more so on the psychological and cultural elements needed for animal domestication and question could these attributes apply to human cultures as well.

Pleasant Disposition

One of the things African people are known for is their pleasant disposition. Chapter XXI of a book titled *Six Months in Ascension* (1878) by Isobel Black Gill talks about an encounter on Ascension Island (located in between Brasil and the Kongo in the Atlantic Ocean) with some of, what the narrator calls, Kroomen. Kroomen were African sailors recruited locally in the British Royal Navy during the nineteenth and twentieth centuries, who were experienced fisherman from the Kru ethnic group of Sotta Krou, which is now Liberia West Africa. The Kru people are also one of the greatest resisters to European colonialism in Africa's history (it's worth looking them up). The author goes on to state:

> We became deeply interested in the history and character of these men—whose industry, honesty, and imperturbable good-nature make them such valuable servants. Physically, the Kroomen are well-formed; of a medium height, and stoutly built, with woolly pates, and of an open, *pleasant countenance*, black-very black, though it be. (emphasis mine)

Having a pleasant disposition is so important to African people that, according to George B. N. Ayittey, it was a part of the Indigenous African Constitution. In his book *Africa Betrayed,* pg. 329, he gives an indigenous constitution derived from oral tradition and under the "Nature of Government" he states:

> The people, the source of all power, shall be governed by a chief (not a
> soldier), chosen by the founding or ancestral lineage. This criteria must be
> combined with others such as intelligence, bravery and a *pleasant*
> *disposition...* (emphasis mine)

Although this is a characteristic to be desired, our general "niceness" contributed heavily to our downfall. Our general kindness and respect for human life was a major cause of the land takeover in Africa. In his book *Of Water and the Spirit,* pages 41-42, Dr. Malidoma Some shows just how the Dagara people's humaneness contributed to them being colonized in Africa. One of the Dagara elders recalls:

> A long, long time ago, the whites came into the land of our people and
> waged war against us...Then one day, one of the men who guarded the
> women's secret hiding place came and told us a strange story. He said
> some white men were in the women's quarters giving them food,
> medicine, and clothing. The messenger himself was clothed like a white
> man. We were confused about what to do, for our law says that you do
> not hurt someone unless they hurt you. A war council was ordered and
> we agreed to make peace with the enemy. Oh, woeful decision, fools as
> we all were! No demands were made, no compromises decided, we sim-
> ply ended the war by refusing to fight.

I think this, and countless other stories, sheds some valuable light on how we may in the future need to shut off this feature of African culture (as needed) to protect our livelihood.

Growth Rate

Large, generally docile mammals who then take years to mature, can also be ruled out. To be economically viable, domesticated animals should grow quickly and reach their full potential within a few years. This criteria rules out elephants, for example, who can take up to fifteen years to reach adult size. At heart, domestication has an economic incentive, and some propositions are better than others. Cattle take just two or three years to mature. – Jared Diamond

African men and women were put to work as early as eight years of age (in Jamaica as early as four). In order for American slavery to be cost efficient for the slave masters, the slaves had to be put to useful work as early as possible. Being put to work early also helped to socialize the youth into their role as property to the business owners.

Although human beings do not grow as fast as most animals, this was overshadowed by the fact that the human commodity could live and work for 40 plus years. The overall long-term investment yielded greater results than could a normal animal whose life expectancy was not as lengthy. Thus, the varying ages overlapped and kept the operation running "smoothly."

Happy to Breed in Captivity

The ancient Kmtjw (Egyptians) were known for their pet cheetahs. They were, however, unable to breed successfully in captivity because cheetahs have elaborate mating rituals, which include running over long distances. This is obviously problematic for zoo keepers as space is vastly reduced in the confines of a menagerie.

African slavery (domestication), however, was successful (unlike the cheetah) due to forced "breeding." This saved individual business owners from actually going across seas to "steal" more Africans. However, the birth rate for slaves was low due to various diseases, work exhaustion, and malnutrition, and this often "forced" European slave owners to seek more imported slaves as the domestic slaves couldn't produce children fast enough.

Now, I am fully aware of the many documented examples of resistance by African captives, and I do acknowledge them. However, what cannot be denied is that the overwhelming majority of African people in the Americas accepted their enslavement and did not attempt to revolt (otherwise it wouldn't have lasted so long). Also, while I would say that African people were not "happy" to breed in captivity, we did nonetheless, and our continual birthing of more "slaves" is one of the reasons why we made such "perfect servants" for European people.

Social Hierarchy

According to the producers of The Animal Attraction,

> "With the exception of the cat, all the major domesticants are group animals used to operating in a dominance hierarchy with strong leadership. To get compliance, all the human has to do is insert him or herself into the social structure—preferably at the top!"

This speaks to the communal nature of our social structures and the acceptance of outsiders within our social sphere. One of the things that has upset me the most about African people is how we are so quick to allow persons of other ethnic groups into our social circles and allow them into the high ranks of our organizations. Our problem is we expect other human beings to act like human beings and we expect them to have the same courtesies that we have. We are too accepting of people.

Because of this, we can never have an organization that is strictly for us. Some may see this as being separatist, but throughout our history we have seen that our downfall was caused by allowing European (or Arab) people into our social hierarchy. This by no means negates native co-conspirators, and any problems that have or would have come if left to our own devices. It, however, speaks about how more devastating it is for outsiders to infiltrate our ranks with hidden agendas than it is for a "domestic" threat to do so. Dr. Chancellor Williams, in his seminal work *The Destruction of Black Civilizations*, articulated this throughout his book. This was the reason for the downfall of ancient Kmt (Egypt) and the strategy has not changed since.

The question is, "Why haven't we learned our lesson if they keep employing the same tactics to destroy us?" How can you radically oppose a people when you have those who belong and are loyal to their ethnic group and heritage in your ranks? This is probably one of the reasons the NAACP isn't as effective as it could be: its major supporters, from inception to the present, have always been European people. This was the center of the beef between W.E.B. Dubois and Marcus Garvey.

On another note, I have always had a problem with accepting European people in Black Greek-lettered organizations. It's nothing against White people (for the sake of them being White), but these organizations were created to be a support network for African/Black people because of the hostile social dynamics of the United States during early Jim Crow. How can you mount an effective campaign against European hegemony when the next president of your organization could be White? You can't deny them the position if they worked hard to earn it. What is the benefit of European people joining these organizations if they already have countless organizations and a political and educational system that reaffirms who they are? Power recognizes power and you can't get power while being dependent on your opposition to provide you with the resources for your liberation.

When other people outside of your culture and heritage are allowed in your sphere of influence, then there is a tendency to shape the goals and aspirations of the organization to that which fits their ideals on how it should function. There is nothing wrong with that, but it can pose a problem because their interests may not coincide with the needs of the organization's core constituency. We have seen this before when functions we created to celebrate African-American heritage and accomplishments are turned into "diversity" programs. Our cultural elements are diluted and lost in this thing called "multi-culturalism" (Black Graduation on the campus of Texas State's majority white campus is such an example). Organizational constitutions are rooted in its founding ethnic heritage. The philosophy that motivates the organization's members comes from a deep ethical tradition that is rooted in the dominant culture from which it sprang.

Black people attempted to change the dynamics of how the United States operated because our cultural heritage said you shouldn't oppress human beings and that you should be fair and create the conditions so that each human being within your borders has the opportunity to reach their full human potential. Anyone familiar with the Civil Rights Movement should know how much of a stir that ideology caused. Our rich tradition in moral ethics clashed with the European "concept" of morality and progress and it caused friction between the two groups.

Conclusion

These characteristics are not the sole reasons for African enslavement in the Americas. This is just my own hypothesis of why African people seemed easier to enslave than those of other ethnic groups. It is plausible because although African people consist of hundreds of different ethnic groups, the overwhelming majority of these groups share the same philosophical concepts, which can truthfully be called "African Culture."

This admittedly is an over simplification of the possibilities as it does not discuss the nature of the skills the Africans possessed that attracted the European enslavers; our resistance to certain diseases the indigenous Indians could not fight off; our lack of advanced weaponry to successfully ward off European colonialism; and our reliance on external spiritual beings to fight our battles. Although our humanity is our greatest gift to the world, it has also been the source of our downfall. I think in this day and age we need to learn from our past. Although we may not want to, for the sake of our health and children, we have to learn to say NO!

Never Let Your Enemy
Become Your Deity

In a recent community forum, I was engaged in a debate concerning a topic that has been discussed in various discourses since the inception of modern psychology: influence vs. control. The discussion, at one point, centered on whether the actions of African-Americans are that of their own will, or if someone else is pulling their cognitive strings. Can the "bad" that Blacks do in America be the result of some external forces? By the same train of thought, can the "good" also be attributed to some external agency as well? Some of the forum members alleged that influence and control are the same thing and did not see a difference in terminology. Articulating the various points and differences took up the bulk of the discussion.

To further inform the reader on the specifics of the conversation, the oppositional view (that other than the author's) suggested that Americans of European ancestry are the only ones capable of influencing and controlling the behavior of African-Americans. I came to this conclusion because throughout the discussion, the members on the other side of the debate never suggested that we had this capability and never provided evidence that we've used this same technique to our advantage.

It seemed as if they were positing that African-American people were not capable of developing their own thoughts, values, standards and actions, and that all of our "negative" behavioral traits can be traced to Europeans controlling our actions, primarily through the media and pop culture.

This author does not walk within this paradigm and firmly asserts that influence and control are not the same thing and that it is impossible to "control" human behavior as there is always the issue of choice. Too many times we give super human powers to European people and even in our attempts to break free from their world view, we often fall into the trap of Euro-centricity, which asserts that their ontological perspective is the norm and any other world view is either deviant or can only be validated in comparison to European values. This essay is an attempt to help others break free from this stronghold, which prevents African-Americans from realizing their full human potential.

Influence vs. Control

Before one can engage in intelligent dialogue, the key terminology of the discussion must be clearly defined and agreed upon as anything else will cause confusion. At the center of the community discussion was the belief that influence and control are the same thing. This goes against common orthodoxy and in many ways the terms are oppositional to each other.

Influence is the ability to cause a change in direction or focus by subtle application of energy. It is not about brute force. It is about learning to bring people in alignment with you by drawing them willingly into your way (Denis). Here, authority and power is GRANTED to the wielder by the one being influenced. Case in point, in indigenous African societies, elders are held with great esteem and reverence. If an elder asks someone of younger age to do something, the younger will more than likely comply out of respect and reverence for the elder. The elder doesn't have to use force for the young person to act in accordance to his will. The person ALWAYS has the choice to comply or not. The wielder uses techniques or situations that will MORE THAN LIKELY get the results he desires.

The concept of control implies complete and direct power over something. It is the ability to cause a definite and immediate result every time through the exertion of your will (Denis). Here, power and authority is TAKEN by the wielder. Control here is applied usually to inanimate objects (resources, schedules, inventory, materials, systems, money, etc), not human perspective or actions. You cannot control thoughts, feelings, desires and basic motivations.

By these definitions, it is hard to fathom how one could equate one with the other: one requires willing participation and the other denies choice (as in the case of rape). This was not the author's first time discussing this topic. This subject has been the focal point of debate many times, and this author has noted a pattern in the majority of those who believe that influence and control are synonymous and that human behavior can be controlled: their belief system is rooted deeply in the Abrahamic religious philosophies

(Judaism, Christianity, & Islam).

While this is not an attack on these religions, it is an observation of how powerful our religious ideology shapes our world view. I call it the "Pharaoh syndrome." All three religions above are rooted in what is called the "Old Testament." In the Old Testament, Moses is sent by God to rescue the enslaved Jewish people in Egypt. God, on purpose, hardens Pharaoh's heart to prevent him from using his human faculties so God could make a point and rescue the Jewish people. In the end, God not only controls the thought process and actions of the Pharaoh, but also punishes him by death for "his" actions towards God's people. From this story and many others comes the belief that super natural powers control human thinking, values and behavior. I will point out later how this is rooted in Euro-centric religious ideology and is foreign to traditional African psychology.

An issue of perspective rooted in one's culture

Every person's philosophical world view is rooted in his culture. As one grows into an adult, certain social norms may change over time, but the core symbology of the language and values are forever present in the subconscious. For those of us of African descent who reside in the United States of America, our education and values have been shaped by a Euro-centric world view. Any behavior that deviates from the model (middle class Caucasian male of European descent) is seen as "pathological." Baldwin (1976: 8) observes:

> The traditional social pathology view of Black behaviors is therefore based on a European conception or definition of reality, or more precisely, a European distortion of reality of Black people. Its rise to prominence in the psychological literature, naturally then, merely reflects the vested social power of Euro-American psychology (and white people generally in European American culture) to legitimate European definitions of reality rather than the necessary objective credibility appeal of its presumed validity.

One of the members in the community discussion, spoken of earlier, suggested that Black people's thoughts and values, en masse, are the result of European hegemony amplified by popular media.

The subject that eventually led to this discussion was centered on the Black man's taste in women and the overall standard of beauty for women, which some in the forum said was being set and enforced by European men who control mass media. Members of the younger generation (which I consider myself a part of) who were present at the discussion table agreed, to a certain extent, with the assumption. We agreed that the media does shape what we think is "hot" and what we think is not. But where we differed is on how long this "influence" lasts in the minds of our people. Is this influence permanent or can it be changed as one matures? We also did not agree that the media controls the minds of the people who experience it. Our conviction is that the people dictate what's hot, and the media amplifies it, but shapes it to its own values (hip hop for instance).

Our conviction was that "Sure, at a young age, we may have found the women on television (light skinned, long haired, skinny women or white woman) attractive. But as we began to come of age and began to see the world through our own lens, (and saw all those naturally fine sistas on the block) the media didn't have such a stronghold on our taste and values." At some point, we believe, human beings come to trust their own value system more so than the popular media. Others may not come to grips with this ever, but it is definitely not the majority.

If you ask the average Black man for his definition of a beautiful woman, I can almost guarantee you that it will include some brown skinned, thick lipped, shapely woman with a big butt: not some skinny, pale, no-shaped woman you find in the magazines. Anyone familiar with Sir Mix-a-lot's song, "Baby Got Back," should understand this sentiment exactly [This author sees this song as a conscious, uplifting song, although it is very derogatory–contradictory? Yes].

Akbar (2004:57) notes that:

> The use of this Eurocentric reference point by non-European (Caucasian) observers has resulted in many non-Caucasian observers having become advocates of their own inferiority. It is for this reason that many so-called "black psychologists" have been identified with the same racist tradition that has characterized the majority of Western psychology and its research findings. Such findings have obsessively dealt with the alleged self-rejection, inferior intellect, defective families and contorted motivations of

African-Americans.

One of the major critiques of "Black Psychology," as expressed by Jackson (1979), is that its very existence confirms their (Europeans) reality as the reality and flaunts statements of their supremacy as [a] scientifically based "fact" (Akbar 2004: 57). Unfortunately, African people have fallen into the myth that Europeans are super natural—that their powers are beyond human capabilities—and they have even amassed enough power that they can control a whole nation of people without the people's consent or participation. Some further believe that to effectively deal with Europeans is going to take another more powerful super natural force (especially in the ideology of the Hebrew Israelites and The Nation of Islam)

This viewpoint assumes several things: 1) human beings do not have free will; 2) if free will exists, only European people have it; 3) Black people are zombies, mere puppets, and are not mentally capable of resisting European hegemony in the world of ideas, values and tastes; and 4) Any attempts to free ourselves from the social Matrix is really a trick by the Europeans to make us think we are actually fighting when we are not (Rene Descartes' Evil Deceiver). If the above assumptions are true, then the works of Harriet Tubman, Fredrick Douglas, Elijah Muhammad, Marcus Garvey, Fannie Lou Hamer, Malcolm X, Martin Luther King Jr., and Paul Robeson are mere myths and their efforts had no affect on shifting the consciousness of African people in America.

Time Orientation

Part of the reason this philosophy permeates so greatly in our psyche is because of our different orientation towards time. As Akbar (2004: 69) has pointed out, "Time is such a powerfully subjective factor that people seldom consider that their time orientation is actually idiosyncratic." The European approach to time is predominantly futuristic. Time is to be quantified and is a scarce resource. Their rhythm is exceedingly urgent and pressured and they are constantly on a mission to "catch-up" with the future. The objectives of their study are focused on the goal of prediction and control (Akbar 2004: 69). In other words, they operate on the basis that if they can predict future events, they can control the initial situations to get the desired outcome they wish. This can be seen in the way they operate in the stock market, in psychology, sociology, advertising and marketing. They are always on a quest to see if they can control people's minds into seeing things their way (in other words, it's a mission to make you buy their products).

Because this way of thinking dominates the popular culture, some of our leaders assume they are actually successful at their attempts at prediction and control. Because of the nature of free will and choice, it is impossible to control what human beings do, so the only thing one can do is try to wield as much influence as possible. American mass media has wielded strong influential power, but this influence is not a permanent fixation on human behavior and is rendered worthless when confronted with someone who has a value system opposite of what the media is advertising (try selling a Big Mac to a Hindu).

We understand that the dominant objective is control here in America. African people typically are not concerned with controlling the future. Our orientation is the past and present (Nobles 1980, Mbiti 1970) (which sometimes works to our detriment). It is very elastic and is reckoned by phenomena.

The Problem Is Choice

When Neo met the Architect in the Matrix Reloaded film, he was introduced to the reality that he has been on this journey several times before and that the concept of the "One" was really an illusion. The Architect (the builder of the Matrix) attempted to build a "perfect" world for human beings to live in, but quickly realized that perfection, in this sense, is an impossibility given the quintessential characteristic that make humans human: freewill.

As long as human beings have two or more options for anything, the concept of European hegemony on the world of ideas, tastes and values is an illusion. As the philosopher James Allen contends, "*All that a man achieves and all that he fails to achieve is the direct result of his own thoughts. In a justly ordered universe, where loss of equipoise would mean total destruction, individual responsibility must be absolute. A man's weakness and strength, purity and impurity, are his own and not another man's.*" In other words, you can't blame someone else for your actions.

As mentioned before, this notion that super natural forces control the decisions of human beings is rooted in the Abrahamic religious philosophy. In traditional African philosophy this is not the case. Karenga (2006: 246), in his discussion of the ancient Egyptian concept of MAAT and its moral applications, states that:

> A fourth basic concept in Maatian moral anthropology is the free will of
> humans. The ground of free will is in divine endowment, but it is further
> supported by Maatian concepts of: 1) malleability of human nature and
> 2) the absence of an overriding concept of fate.

The locus classicus of this philosophy can be seen in the Coffin Text 1130
in which the Creator lists Four Good Deeds. I will quote it in its entirety to
give a contextual basis for the free will concept:

> I did Four Good Deeds within the portals of the horizon
> I made the four winds so that every man might breathe there from in his
> time (and place). This is the First Deed.

> I made the great flood waters so that the humble person might benefit
> from it like the great. This is the Second Deed.

> *I made every man like his fellow.* **I did not command that they do evil. It
> was their hearts that violated what I had said.** This is the Third Deed.

> And I caused that their hearts not forget The West in order that divine
> offerings might be made to the divine powers of the provinces. This is
> the Fourth Deed (CT VII, 461-465) (emphasis mine).

As can be seen by the statement, "I made every man like his fellow," the
Egyptians believed that human kind possessed the same mental faculties and
capabilities. The second part of the Third Deed affirms that in the minds of
the ancient Africans, it is man's choice to do good (Maat) or evil (Isfet) and
is not the result of some super natural force as expressed in the Christian
myth of Moses. This philosophy is common all throughout Africa and is
even the basis of the Indian and East Asian spiritual systems. So the idea that
another man or force can control your behavior or thoughts is not in align-
ment with traditional African philosophy.

No matter how strong the influence, you always have a choice. If a rob-
ber puts a gun to your face and says give me your money or I will kill you,
you still have a choice in this situation. You can either: 1) give him the money

and live, or 2) refuse, fight back and possibly be killed by the assailant. Even though the gun is a strong motivating force, its presence does not eliminate one's options. So the idea that European people, through the power of media, control our tastes, values and perceptions is ludicrous because we all still have an alternative world view we can choose from. It is our job to recognize the alternatives and use it to our advantage—in other words, exercise our mental muscles.

Conclusion

Oftentimes in the struggle for African liberation, we limit the affects of our efforts by lowering one's own capabilities, potential, self-worth and historical achievement, while at the same time elevating and giving power to that which one is in opposition to. You cannot effectively mount a strategy of resistance if you honestly believe your enemies are Gods: that their capabilities are divine and there's nothing you can do about it (Al Queda definitely doesn't have this mentality).

In the Matrix Reloaded film, two of the agents sent to kill Neo spotted him at a secret meeting. Before engaging Neo in a battle, the agents reminded themselves that Neo is "only human." Although Neo in Matrix I displayed many God-like powers, the agents understood the nature of the Matrix and knew that regardless of Neo's powers, he was still a human being whose fate is just like the rest of humanity. Although this is a film, movies convey deep, philosophical views on the nature of reality and are a projection of the creative faculties of its creator, and more specifically, his cultural core. We need to have the mentality the agents in the Matrix possessed when dealing with European hegemony. We must remember that they are only human and are subject to the same laws of the universe as African-Americans.

Their power (or perceived power) is realized in the cohesiveness of their culture and the strength in their numbers. African people have proven time and time again that we change the course of history when we unite in great numbers for a cause. Why do we need to reinvent the wheel? If we want to change the perspective of what is beautiful in mass media, we need to collectively present beauty from our perspective to the masses with no apologies.

One of the major damaging events in our recent history was the forced adoption of Christianity during the transatlantic slave period. We were given images of what God looked like and he looked like the very men who enslaved us. How can you fight a people who look like God? That event told us subconsciously that "It is pointless to resist as they are in the image of God. So to resist them is to resist God. So Black people are going to need a God to fight off their God."

From this point on, in the words of Ashra Kwesi, *we let our enemy become our deity*. And this slave mentality has penetrated the minds of African people to the present day. But luckily we had our own Neos who were unplugged from the Matrix and realized their own powers. These people helped to set others free: Harriet Tubman, Nat Turner, Frederick Douglass, WEB DuBois, Gabriel Prosser, Denmark Vessy, Cinque, and many others.

Europeans aren't the only ones who can own a television station, a radio station, a magazine, calendars, books, film, etc. We give them too much credit, and the illusion that they run things is ever present because we WILL-INGLY give them such power. Who shut down a city's mass transit system for a year without the use of weapons or intimidation tactics? We did! Who in the midst of Jim Crow had movie theatres, hotels, banks, construction companies, radio stations, and hospitals? We did! Who flew dozens of missions during World War II and didn't lose a plane? We did! Who marched on Washington by the thousands and informed the world about the atrocities of living within U.S. borders and changed the course of legislative history? We did! There is nothing we can't do if we believe it can be done. Our ancestors already showed us how to do it. You just have to make the choice to follow in their footsteps and expand their vision, or take the blue pill and continue an existence where ignorance is bliss. Ye are Gods: it's about time you believed it.

James Allen gives a unique perspective on this subject when he states:

It has been usual for men to think and to say, "Many men are slaves because one is an oppressor; let us hate the oppressor!" But there is amongst an increasing few a tendency to reverse this judgment and to say, "One man is an oppressor because many are slaves; let us despise the slaves." The truth is that oppressor and slaves are cooperators in ignorance, and, while seeming to afflict each other, are in reality, afflicting themselves.

A perfect knowledge perceives the action of law in the weakness of the oppressed and the misapplied power of the oppressor. A perfect love, seeing the suffering which both states entail, condemns neither; a perfect compassion embraces both oppressor and oppressed. He who has conquered weakness and has pushed away all selfish thoughts belongs neither to oppressor nor oppressed. He is free.

References:

Akbar, Naim (2004). *Papers In African Pyschology*. Florida, Mind productions & Associates.

Allen, James. *As a Man Thinketh*. Public domain

A. de Buck. (1935-1961). *The Egyptian Coffin Text*. 7 Volumes. Chicago: University of Chicago press.

Denis, David. *Control Vs. Influence*. Freedom Speakers and Trainers. http://www.deliverfreedom.com/view_1848688.html

Jackson, Gerald G. (1979). *The origin and development of black psychology: Implications for black studies and human behavior*. Studia Africana 1, 3, 270-293.

Karenga, Malauna (2006). *MAAT: The moral ideal in Ancient Egypt*. Los Angeles. University of Sankore Press.

Nobles, Wade (1980). *African Philosophy: Foundations for black psychology*. In R. Jones (Ed), Black Psychology. New York: Harper and Row.

Mbiti, John S. (1970). *African religions and philosophy*. Garden City, NY: Anchor Books

Uh Uhh, You Can't Tell Me Nuthin!

Self-Defeatism:
A Roadblock To Your Blessings

I recently met with a client/friend at a local urban restaurant to discuss some business and our plans for the future. Our discussion centered around how best to utilize our gifts and talents in the capacity of helping members in our community reach their full human potential. After showing off my superb skills in the art of sopping chicken tenders in a sea of honey mustard sauce, we began to discuss the monumental task we agreed to tackle and the potential (I say inevitable) bottlenecks we would surely face.

We are two individuals who have lived two totally different lives, but have come to the same conclusions regarding the nature of struggle. Through our expressed ordeals, we noticed that in our everyday interactions with good intentioned people (ones who desire in life to do great things), that a good number of them exhibited a certain behavioral trait we agreed was self-destructive.

Every time they expressed their desires, wants, and goals in life, they would always back-door their aspirations with talk that made it seem like it was impossible to accomplish that which they aspired to do (or a behavioral habit they wanted to change). A lot of these individuals stressed that their lives felt empty (that there was a void) and that they were unhappy either in their relationships, careers, or spiritual commitments. The sentiments weren't that the situations were bad, but either they didn't think they could change the mundacity of it all or they feared the responsibility the success of their endeavors would bring.

The issue at hand is *self-defeatism*. Self-defeatism is a self-resistance to change. It is a series of voices in your head that try to prevent you from confronting your shortcomings. It prevents a person from learning the lessons in every experience. You have seen it hundreds of times in your life. When a person says to you, "I desire to be rich, but I don't think it will happen in my lifetime." Or, "I know I'm jealous but I don't think I can change." Or, "I want to make a change in the world, but I don't think my contribution will make a big difference." Or, "We need to control the distribution of our products in the Black community, but the White man isn't going to let that happen." Their goals will never be realized because they have allowed the energy of self-defeatism to stop the race before they've had a chance to come out the blocks.

Self-defeatism is a black whole that sucks the life out of a human being, and when left unchecked, can lead one on a journey through disappointment, depression, food/alcohol/drug abuse, violence, murder, and ultimately suicide. For me, this is not something people should take lightly. Life is meant to be lived and lived abundantly. Our thinking alone can block access to channels that lead to great blessings and wisdom. A single self-defeating behavior (or single life-enhancing behavior) will not be noticeable or have a lasting effect. But a series of self-defeating behaviors (again left unchecked) will bring about physical illness, anxiety, nervous breakdowns and in the most extreme cases, death. However, the adoption and practice of a series of life-enhancing behaviors over time can lead to a breakthrough that comes when our mind, body and spirit are integrated into a wholeness that becomes a source of our creativity, insight, usefulness and contentment.

My friend and I would run into people who would think, "I am not good enough and people won't accept me unless I am better." The question ultimately for us was, "How can very motivated people (like ourselves) better motivate others to see the power, the genius, the greatness they possess within themselves?" The answer to this question is more difficult to calculate than one may expect. Maybe it is because of my young age (28), or maybe it's because I am a Leo (they say we are TOO confident and overly motivated—but that's all hearsay), but I can't grasp what it is that makes people like this.

My friend and I discussed how we would get frustrated with other human beings who did not realize the potential we obviously saw in them. But we had to realize that being a good friend (a vitalist) requires patience and allowing others to march to their own drum beat (You can't push a river to go with the flow). There is no way you can "talk" someone into realizing their greatness. Only a life changing situation, in which they are forced to experience and reflect on its deeper meanings (lessons), will initiate them into the awareness of themselves.

It's really hard when it involves people who are close to you (spouses, friends and family). Usually people are more willing to take your advice if they don't know you. Why? I have yet to figure this out. But I suspect people believe that because you are close to them, that you are "supposed" to say things that uplift them, so they don't take you seriously. I even had a person tell me one time that they hate calling me because I always have something positive to say about a seemingly bad issue (yeah, that's what I said).

Scientists have even proposed that people are addicted to emotions (caused by neuropeptides) and seek out situations and things that make them have the same emotional responses, even if there are different opportunities that may be better or worse in a real sense (See "What The Bleep Do We Know" documentary). Maybe this is the reason people have self-defeating attitudes towards life? I don't know. But as usual, our ancestors provide great insight into the matter. A Kemetic (Egyptian) proverb states, "It is no use whatever preaching Wisdom to men: you must inject it into their blood." Another proverb states, "A man can't be judge of his neighbor's intelligence. His own vital experience is never his neighbor's." These proverbs got me to thinking more deeply about the subject and it made more sense when I came across these other Kemetic teachings:

1. True teaching is not an accumulation of knowledge; it is an awakening of consciousness that goes through successive stages.

2. What reveals itself to me ceases to be mysterious for me alone: if I unveil it to anyone else, he hears mere words which betray the living sense: Profanation, but never revelation.

3. Each truth you learn will be, for you, as new as if it had never been written.

4. Every man must act in the rhythm of his time ... such is wisdom.

So I get the message ancestors: just let people be(Simba Simbi); they will get it on their own. I just wish more people would realize the great gifts they posses inside and that these gifts are there to be utilized in the greatest capacity possible. The fear of failure or unhappiness should not deter one from experiencing the best life has to offer and their past triumphs should be motivators for future endeavors.

I remember T.D. Jakes saying one time, "Extraordinary things ONLY happen to extraordinary people" (What you don't know CAN hurt you - Extraordinary things, Extraordinary People - Tape 3). The hardships that one faces and overcomes gives certain people a stronger sense of faith that makes them more optimistic about life than people who haven't gone through as much struggle. Don't let your pessimism, doubting vocabulary and wondering about "what ifs" block your blessings before they've had a chance to manifest. Life is meant to be lived more abundantly and the only thing the creator requires from you is faith—a belief/conviction that things will be alright (real easy to say when you aren't going through something).

Ultimately, I can only control my thoughts and actions. I can't get frustrated that other people do not have the same motivation and zeal for life that I have (on some things, cuz I'm actually lazy as hell). I believe wholeheartedly that "What humans have done, humans can do." All human beings are made up of the same essence—the power and the love of God—and with the realization that God is my primary ancestor, at this stage in my life, "YOU CAN'T TELL ME NUTHIN!" laaa laa la laaaah...

Kemetic Proverb Notes

Massey, Gerald. (2004). *Ancient Egypt the Light of the World*, Volume I, Nuvision Publications

Schwaller de Lubicz, Ihsa. (1978). *Her-Bak: The Living Face of Ancient Egypt*. Inner Traditions

Schwaller de Lubicz, Ihsa. (1978). *Her-Bak: Egyptian Initiate*. Inner Traditions

The BIGGEST Fear In A Relationship!

My colleagues and I, I think, are some of the most profound philosophers the world has yet to discover. When we get together, somehow the conversation will shift from who won the Nas and Jay-Z battle to the integrity of the hypothesis of extra dimensional realities in the new found M-Theory in Quantum Mechanics. We don't skip a beat when it comes to our philosophical rantings and we can argue, literally, from sun up 'til sun up about whose perspective is the most sound. This is one of the reasons why we don't hang out much: we won't get anything done (like bathe, eat, change our children's diapers, you know the little things).

Every now and then we will descend from the discussion of the deeper significance of the Matrix films in comparison to African ontological philosophy and metaphysics, to discuss something more close to home that everyone can relate to: relationships. I am one of the few in my posse [do they still say posse these days?], who isn't married or has ever been married; so I am like the majority of you reading this article who have a 100% failure rate at relationships. My many, shame to say, relationships have allowed me to experience all types of women and scenarios. So my bachelor status and ideology in conversation with a group of married men and women makes for an interesting discussion.

The last discussion centered on our biggest fears in relationships. What are people so afraid of in relationships? Is it the commitment? The fear of losing a sense of individuality? The fear that someone else in the world could be better for me and if I hold off just a little bit longer maybe I could find them? What has people running from the nature of relationships?

After throwing around some "thee-sus-ses" (inside joke) in our best Cornel Westian linguistico slang, the conversation went deeper and more specific as to the nature of jealousy. What makes people jealous in relation-

ships? What can be done to curb a partner's jealous thoughts and moods?
Does jealousy play a positive role in relationships?

It is hard trying to answer these questions from a balanced perspective,
especially since men don't get jealous. Now the sistas in the conversation
vehemently disagreed and claimed to have some silly things like police
reports to back up their claim: something about most stalkers are
men...hmph! Until I see some empirical data on the subject matter my posi-
tion still stands.

But seriously, jealousy is a big issue in relationships and I argue it is the
source of our greatest relationship fear: losing someone we care about
deeply. Actually, to me, jealousy is more a symptom of something deeper
rather than a source. The question is what deeper lies at the heart of jealousy
beyond certain events that might trigger the emotional response? Usually
jealousy is associated with the fear that your partner might like or love some-
one else more than you because some third partner may have some physical
or personality traits that may not be as expressive in your physique or char-
acter.

Jealousy is a natural response and defense mechanism when one feels
some third party is infiltrating the sacred relationship space. Sure, we can all
be like, "You should just trust your partner and if you don't 'got' trust, what
do you have?" We all know from experience that some jealous tendencies are
warranted given some human beings act on their thoughts of infidelity. But
I argue that the assumption must be based on something solid and not sim-
ply your insecurities.

What I argue is at the heart of jealousy is not that your mate will like or
love someone else more than you, but that someone else will recognize your
mate's inner gifts and affirm more than you the value of who they are as a
human being. So the fear really isn't rooted in your mate, but the possibility
that someone else outside of the relationship could bring out the best in
your mate and that he/she might take that as a cue to leave.

One thing, and I don't care who you are, a person can't stand is when their
mate is having a good time with someone of the opposite sex. Ain't nothing
wrong with someone making them laugh, but they "bet not" be laughing and
having a good time with somebody else more than they with do you. If your
mate sees your face light up when one of your friends of the opposite sex
enters the room, it's over. A more serious "threat" for couples, and especial-
ly among women, is that friend who you can talk about anything with. This
is the person who you can confide in about relationship problems, spiritual

issues, philosophy in The Last Dragon film or just vent about the work day. This motha-&*% gots to go. It's an issue of intimacy and no one is supposed to be close to my wo/man more than me!

For me, what is at the heart of this jealousy is the fear someone else will understand and appreciate your mate more than you. I had a friend who told me about one of her friends who was cheating on his girlfriend with another woman. She asked her friend why was he doing it and he replied:

> With her I can be myself. I don't have to walk on egg shells wondering if
> I'm going to offend her or make her angry in some manner. When I'm over
> her house, she doesn't trip that I kick my shoes off and relax. She makes me
> feel like a king and I am glad to return the royal treatment. (paraphrased)

I am by no means condoning his actions, but we must remember that not everyone cheats to satisfy their sexual urge: it is something deeper that needs to be addressed. But at the heart of his statements was the fact that with the other woman, he felt she allowed him to be himself around her and because she recognized the spirit of who he is, she treated him in a manner that brought the best out of him (although cheating is not a worthy trait to posses).

In a relationship we need to be reaffirmed as to who we are. If a person can't be him/herself (flaws and all) with you, then they may seek out that affirmation elsewhere. What we want to do is create an environment in which we constantly reaffirm the true spirit and gifts our mates possess. When we are able to sustain such an environment, then I think we can curb jealous tendencies in our relationships. For some reason we feel that once we have a person that's it, no more work needs to be done. He/she should just be grateful to be with all of this wonderfulness and just knowing that I'm with them should be enough for them to be secure. Relationships do not work like that.

We have to remember in America we are at a disadvantage. We no longer live in communities that are created to be a support network for couples. So couples are forced to try and be everything to each other and for me, it is the reason for most relationship failures. So in this absence of a community network of people who are genuinely concerned about the nature of your relationship (a community of folk who view a problem in your relationship as a problem for the whole community structure), we have to do what we can to be a support network for our mates.

Now, personally, I think the underlying fear associated with jealousy is really rooted in selfishness. We want our mate's vital energy and gifts to only be recognized, utilized and brought about by ourselves, and when we feel someone else recognizes it, we go into selfish mode, trying to keep our mate to ourselves as a possession. But if your mate has a gift (be it in council, in the arts, or problem solving), you should understand that their gifts are meant to be shared with the community and you can't get jealous every time someone other than you wants to utilize those gifts. Your mate belongs to the community as well…but this does not mean your bed either for all of you heathens reading this.

Just go home right now and hug and kiss your mate and show them how much you appreciate them. Let them know in your own unique way that you recognize who they are and you value all of the great gifts they possess. I think if both people do this, then there is no room for jealousy: he/she knows where home is.

Dedication

Geneology of Harold Johnson III (Asar Imhotep)

I decided to do something kind of unconventional by ending this work with the dedication rather than putting it in the beginning. There is a Kemetic proverb that states:

> "If you would know yourself, take yourself as starting point and go back to its source; your beginning will disclose your end."

This work has primarily been a discourse on "Asar Imhotepian" philosophy. This work is, however, grounded in the notion that we stand on the shoulders of those who have come before us. So I decided to start with me and work my way backwards, ending with my family, in an effort to better know who I am. We are on a lifetime quest to answer for ourselves: Who am I? Where did I come from? What is my purpose? What must I do to fulfill that purpose? I personally feel that you can't honestly know who you are without having some sense of who your family is.

It is African protocol to be able to name your family members at least seven generations going back. Knowing a little about your family and what went on in their lives allows you to better understand the social norms, traditions and circumstances you are presently in. It can also serve as a means of empowerment and inspiration knowing that you belong to a lineage that has contributed to human flourishing in some manner. This dedication was placed here to inspire you, if you haven't, to go back and start a record of your own lineage so your future family members will have an accurate account of their history. I take great pride in partaking in this endeavor and by the time I do another work I will better be able to put more pieces to the puzzle together.

At this stage it has been very difficult for many African people in the Diaspora to collect information about their ancestors because of the Trans Atlantic Slave Holocaust. I have definitely run into this problem while trying to piece together my family history. But what I have discovered thus far has been phenomenal and I encourage everyone to find out who you are through your lineage and then create written records of your investigations. This is by no means the ending of my research, and I will continue to bring to light the legacy that goes back to the first occasion (Sp-Tpy). The list below is by no means exhaustive of the names and information I currently possess. I would say 75% of my family is from Louisiana (New Orleans, Baton Rouge and Opelousas). My dad's side of the family is all from Louisiana and my grandfather's family on my mother's side is all from Louisiana. From the records it was very common for my family members to have no less than nine children, all the way up to 16. All I can say is if you are a Thompson, King or Chenier in Louisiana, 12 times out of 10 we are related (which is why I can't date anyone from Louisiana).

I dedicate this work to my family, those whom I've met and those whom I haven't, but who communicate with me through dreams and nature. To those ancestors whose names are unknown to me, who now reside in the *Zamani*, whose wisdom to this date continues to influence contemporary thought and whose sense of humanity and ethical grounding has laid the foundation for morality and human flourishing, this work is devoted to your memory. And to the youth who march onward and upward toward the *light*, this book is respectfully dedicated.

Harold James Johnson III: Born in Jacksonville, FL, July 30, 1979.
Children: *Elijah Heru Johnson* born April 7, 2004.
Parents: *Cynthia Elaine Foster* and *Harold Johnson Jr.* (Brother of Daphne Washington)
Siblings: *Mary* (died at birth), *Tyrone, Sean, Christopher* and *Joseph.*
Maternal Side: *Cynthia Foster* (Brother of *Joseph Foster*) is the daughter of *Baptiste Joseph Foster* [Born June 20, 1933] and *Joann Green.* Baptiste's parents are *Una Cecile Philips* and *David Charles Foster Sr.* [Died 1956 in New Orleans]. Una's parents are *Willie and Ellen Philips.* At this point I cannot go any further on my mother's father's side. My Grandmother, *Joann Green,* has five siblings: *Mitchell, Judy, Beatye, Eddie* and *Barbara Green.* Their parents were *Eddie* and *Dorthy Green.* Ed's mother's name is *Ida (Jackson)Green* and she *Dorthy's* mother is *Josie Jackson.* This is as far as I can go on my mother's mother's side.

Paternal Side: My father's parents are *Harold James Hughes Johnson Sr.* and *Rose Thomas*. At this point I have no information on my grandfather's family on my dad's side. But Rose is the daughter of *Mary Genevieve Chenier* [Born April 28, 1910] and *Arthur Thomas* (son of *Joseph Thomas* and *Elizabeth Paul*). Mary's parents are *Mary Madeline King* [Born August 8, 1875 - daughter of *Sylvester King* (later changed his last name to Thomas) and *Genevieve Chretien*] and *Leon Chanier* (Born in 1872 – son of slaves *Celestin Chenier* and *Marie Helen Pierre*).

Ashe!

www.ingramcontent.com/pod-product-compliance
Lightning Source LLC
Chambersburg PA
CBHW021050090426
42738CB00006B/276